# Twinkle Toes

# *Twinkle Toes*

## Tales of a
## Broadway Gypsy
### 1949—1969

# GENE GAVIN

*Edited by Richard Freeman Tuttle*

ISBN: 978-0-9993119-0-5

Books may be purchased by contacting the publisher and author at:
Richard.glendale@gmail.com

*Book and cover design by Deborah Daly*

*Gene Gavin, my uncle,*
*wasn't a star with his name in lights on the Great White Way*
*but he was a star to me*
*and I thank him for giving me his memories.*

# * Chapter 1 *

*I* made my first dramatic debut in Brown City, Michigan, when I interrupted preparations for Christmas dinner in 1930 by deciding to be born while Mom was stuffing the turkey and baking pies. Fast forward through my formative years, however, to the summer between my sophomore and junior years at Flint High School when my older brother and I took the train from Detroit to New York City.

It was love at first sight. We ate at the Horn & Hardart Automat on Forty-Second Street, went to the top of the Empire State Building, took the ferry to the Statue of Liberty, rode the subways, went to the museums, and visited Coney Island where we rode the parachute jump, the roller coaster, and the Ferris wheel. We did all the touristy things, including going to the movies at Radio City Music Hall where we saw *Anna and the King of Siam* with Rex Harrison and Irene Dunn.

One day near the end of our week, I went to Grand Central Station to surprise a friend who was coming on a vacation with his family and did not know that I had come to New York. While waiting for his train to arrive, I went to the men's room. Standing next to me was a man in full bloom. I was dumbfounded. Other than my own, I had never seen an erection. For the next couple of days, until the end of our vacation, I made several trips to see what was being exposed at the urinals of Grand Central Station.

New York had double decker busses in those days. One afternoon I ditched my brother and took a bus up and down Fifth Avenue, mostly for the adventure but also to see the landmarks. I had spread a map over my lap and was checking it to see what I was passing. Gradually I became aware that the hand of the man sitting next to me was under my map. His fingers were creeping towards Union Square. I was embarrassed and excited and did not know what to do. I didn't want to create a scene, but I was also afraid I might stain my trousers and have to finish the day with the map held in front of my crotch. The dilemma was solved when I reached under the map to move his hand away. The man left the bus suddenly. Adventures like this never happened back home in Flint!

We finished our New York City visit with our first Broadway show, *Oklahoma!*, and a revival of *The Red Mill* with Eddie Foy, Jr. When we left on the train, I was already planning my next trip to New York. I'd been bitten by the Manhattan bug. I don't think my brother ever went back.

For the rest of my high school years, I focused on theater. After I discovered that Flint High School subscribed to *The New York Times*, I devoured it everyday, dreaming of theater and dancing and acting. I had found my calling. I was awarded a scholarship to the University of Denver where I planned to major in theater.

After my first term at the University of Denver, I knew Denver wasn't for me. I wanted to be in New York. However, after Christmas vacation in Flint, I went back to Denver on the Greyhound. I saw *Annie Get Your Gun* with Billie Worth in Chicago. In Denver, a road company of *Oklahoma!* was playing at the Auditorium. I snuck backstage to watch several performances, and apparently, I fit in perfectly with the theater world because no one stopped me except a chorus boy who took my virginity.

I had been thinking all this while that if I continued school in Denver, I would end up teaching drama at a high school or college, and that wasn't my goal. I wanted New York. With the impetus of *Oklahoma!*, I decided the quickest way into the theatre would be through dancing. I called Mom and told her I wanted to quit college and go to New York. She must have been disappointed, but she didn't argue. So, I gave up my scholarship, got back on the Greyhound, went to Flint for a few days, then caught another Greyhound to New York.

# ∗ *Chapter 2* ∗

T he second week of January 1949, I arrived in New York at the Thirty-Fourth Street bus station and took a taxi to the Kenmore Hall Hotel on East Twenty-Third Street. I had just turned eighteen, was looking for my entry to "show business," and had not a clue how to go about it.

I had picked the Kenmore Hall out of a brochure from the New York Central Railroad because it advertised a swimming pool. If I was to be a sophisticated New Yorker I might as well have access to a pool. I didn't know it at the time but the Kenmore Hall had a little claim to fame as a former residence of Dashiel Hammet and Nathaniel West. When I arrived, however, it was a residence for a lot of people with physical disabilities. Rooms cost twelve dollars a week and were large enough for a single bed, a wash basin, and a closet. The shared bath was down the hall. The swimming pool in the basement was dank and dreary. I only used it once. There was a masseur there who looked like Sydney Greenstreet and when he asked me if I wanted a massage, I responded in the affirmative, part of my newly found sophistication. But, when he started massaging things that I didn't expect, I beat a quick retreat. I suppose if he had looked like Tyrone Power, I probably would have stuck around for a happy ending.

It was exciting just to wake up in the morning and know that I was in New York. The subway and the busses were a dime, just recently raised from a nickel. Along Broadway from Ninety-Sixth Street to Times Square, movie houses every four or five blocks played second-run films. Most of the once grand brownstones on the West Side were rooming houses where rooms could be rented for ten dollars a week, twelve if they had a refrigerator and a hot plate. The newsstands were an adventure selling morning and afternoon papers. I could choose from *The New York Times*, the *Herald Tribune*, *Daily News*, *Mirror*, *World-Telegraph*, *Sun*, *Post*, *PM*, *Journal-American* or the *Brooklyn Eagle* for three cents. *Variety* cost twenty-five cents but had all the theatrical news. Horn & Hardart's Automat restaurants were everywhere and it never ceased to amaze me that whether you put a dollar or a quarter on the marble counter, the cashier, with a sweep of the hand, would give you the correct change in nickels. I soon learned that you could have a free lemonade at the Automat by using the glasses filled with ice provided for iced tea plus the lemon that sat next to the tea spigot and the sugar shakers that sat on all the tables.

There I was in Times Square, the center of the universe, the crossroads of the world. The latest films played at the Paramount, Capitol, Astor, Victoria, Rivoli, Criterion, Roxy, Mayfair, Gaiety, Loews State, and Palace. Half of these threw in a stage show with the movie. The Astor and Taft Hotels were there. Around the corner on Forty-Second Street were the second run theatres. On the side streets were the legitimate theaters, all of them busy during the height of the season. If a show flopped, another took its place almost immediately. Standing room was fifty cents for matinees and seventy-five cents for evening shows.

The marquees advertised the names of the stars in bright lights—Katherine Cornell, Helen Hayes, Henry Fonda, Paul Muni, Ray Bolger, Ethel Merman, Mary Martin plus new names like Marlon Brando and Julie Harris. It seemed to me that the stars had come to earth to entertain us earthly beings, and I was there and wanted to be a part of it. But, first, I needed a job.

Within a week I found a job at the head offices of JC Penny's on West Thirty-Fourth Street, next door to the Sloane House YMCA. I became a "sortographer" for twenty-eight dollars a week. I sat in a chair with two sliding trays about six feet long on either side of me. Merchandise orders from the thousand Penny's stores across the country were put on a small table in front of me, and I spent the day putting them in their correct folders, sliding the trays back and forth until I found the store numbers. When the tray was full, we filed the orders in their appropriate file drawers. One day in the spring, I was at work and noticed that a fellow employee had a black mark on his forehead. I was about to tell him that his face was dirty when another person arrived with a dirty forehead, just in time for me to realize something was going on. Eighteen years old and I had never seen a mark on a forehead on Ash Wednesday. Maybe the Catholics in Flint did it after school?

In summer, the office was intolerable. It was so hot that I stuck to the seat and was afraid to stand and have my wet bottom show. If the temperature went over ninety, the office would close early. It was always a debate whether you wanted the temperature to rise so that you could get out early or if you would prefer that the thermometer stay down and be more comfortable all day long. I made neither friends nor enemies at the office and was probably considered something of an oddball, living alone in New York City at eighteen.

I lived close enough to the office to be able to walk to work. Every morning, I bought *The New York Times* for three cents and stopped at the Automat for breakfast. At first I bought corn muffins, but after trying English muffins, which I had never seen before, they became my staple. English muffins were ten cents, coffee was a nickel, and orange juice was a dime. Lunch was at Nedick's, a ten-cent hot dog and a five-cent orange drink.

Dinner, I bought at Bickford's or the Automat for a dollar and a quarter. There was no tip necessary at the Automat.

So, within a week I had a job and a place to stay. Now I needed to start on my theatrical career. I knew two names— Hanya Holm and Martha Graham. I looked up Hanya Holm in the telephone book and found that she taught at Michael's, a ratty rehearsal hall on Eighth Avenue that remained there under the name of Fazil's until 2008. The hall was in a building between Forty-Sixth and Forty-Seventh Streets that looked like it was about to collapse. I climbed the rickety stairs to the third floor and found Hanya's secretary in a little cubbyhole of an office. Unfortunately, Hanya only taught classes during the day. She had other teachers teaching the night classes, but I wanted Hanya. Since the place didn't look like my idea of glamorous New York, I decided to move on to the next name I knew.

Back to the phone book to look up Martha Graham. Martha's studio was on Fifth Avenue between Twelfth and Thirteenth Streets, above the Fifth Avenue Cinema. It was a spacious studio with a beautiful hardwood floor, men's and women's dressing rooms, and a private room for Martha. Best of all, they had evening classes starting at five thirty which would allow me to leave work at five, take the subway downtown, walk to the studio, and change in time for class. It was promised that Martha would teach some of them. Classes were a dollar each or ten classes for seven dollars if you bought a card. Mom had agreed to pay for the classes instead of college, so I registered, and every two weeks Mom sent me a check made payable to Martha Graham.

Communication with Mom back in Flint was by mail be-cause phone calls were too expensive and used for emergencies only. My letters were gems: How are you? I am fine. And very little else. Even though I was busy doing and seeing new things all the time, there never seemed to be anything to write about. Once I forgot to write, and the next week I received a blank piece of paper and a stamped envelope. Message received.

A job, a place to stay, and now a place to study, with Martha Graham no less! I was set. And I was in wonderful New York. All I needed was a tee shirt, a dance belt, and a pair of cotton tights or white duck trousers or shorts. No shoes were necessary at Graham's. The dance belt was a bit of a mystery and uncomfortable until I learned that "things" were worn up and not down like in a jock strap. Later, I would hear rumors that certain performers stuffed an old sock in their belts to fill them out.

When I first started at Martha's, she was preparing her company for a tour, so I didn't see her until she returned, but she was always a larger than life presence even when she wasn't there in person. When I saw her dance on that tour, I didn't understand a thing she did, but I took it on faith that I was seeing something extraordinary.

My first teachers at the Martha Graham Studio were Yuriko, a company dancer who was staying home with her new baby while the company went on tour, and Marjorie Mazia, a former company member who was very pregnant. She was married to Woody Guthrie so, you might say, I took some of my first dance classes with her son, Arlo. I have had a lot of tangential relationships with famous people.

The atmosphere at the Martha Graham Studio was intense. There was an intellectual approach full of imagery to the physical medium of dance. It immediately imbued one with a sense of importance to be involved with this art form. Everyday I dashed from work, jumped on the subway, changed my clothes, and sat on the floor waiting for the exercises to begin. The intensity increased when Graham returned from tour and started teaching. Martha was nothing if not theatrical. With her hair swept back in a bun, exposing her magnificent skull, wearing a black gown that looked like a nightie, she would sweep into class spewing philosophy, psychology, sociology, mythology, and factual tidbits on life, politics, theatre, dance, and quotes from obscure people. Citing Gordon Craig, she said "art is not reflection, it's revelation." I bought that and still do. One time, she swept into class as we were sitting on the floor waiting to begin; she sat and started talking to us in a normal voice. As she continued, her voice got lower and lower until it was almost a whisper, and we, on the floor, were almost levitating in order to hear her. Our energy was at fever pitch, and we hadn't done anything yet. She used words like birth and death and loins and passion and redemption. She spoke in imagery and always seemed to find a new way to use a common word, explaining the etymology and meaning. Sometimes, I thought she scoured the dictionary in order to impress us. By the end of class, we were spent physically and emotionally, afraid we were inadequate, but inspired to become otherwise. She was an extraordinary force, and we called her Martha.

Martha had her own technique and vocabulary. Ballet terms were not used. There were a few exceptions— "knee bend" didn't really suffice for *"plié"* and the "barre," although not used much, was still the "barre." The classes started with floor exercises (designed for the female body and terribly difficult for the male physique), then standing exercises, jumps and falls, then steps moving across the floor. After the company returned from tour, members of the company including Erick Hawkins, Helen McGehee, and Robert Cohan, taught some of the classes. At the end of class, I would walk home, have dinner, and go to bed.

As time passed, I began to learn that the modern dance world was fractionalized. I had heard about Doris Humphrey, Charles Weidman, Iris Mabry, Sybil Shearer, and Anna Sokolov. They were all, for the most part, from the same family tree. It started with the Denishawn Dancers as mama and papa, and then the children branched out on their own with their own ideas. Even Jack Cole, the jazz dance choreographer, had been in the Denishawn Company. Hanya was an exception, coming from Mary Wigman in Germany. The other faction had roots in Africa. Katharine Dunham and Pearl Primus had roots in black ethnic dances. As a student, you were expected to cast the die, pledge allegiance, and remain loyal to your branch of the tree. Modern dancers used first names, even with their idols, and ballet was looked down upon.

I also learned that some of my fellow students weren't completely loyal to Martha Graham. They took classes, on the sly, with some of those other big name teachers. Some even took ballet classes. Eventually I snuck off to take a class at the Weidman studio on West Sixteenth Street. The studio was dark and dank and set up like a theatre with a raked stage. To me, Weidman's technique seemed easier and I enjoyed the classes. They were like play time and very "dancy." I was quickly learning my snobbery quite well. The atmosphere at Weidman's was more relaxed with students hanging around after classes and being more social.

I met and was embraced by my first New York social group at Weidman's studio. It was one of the best times of my life. None of us, except one, had any money. The one who had money was happy to play the generous Bohemian. He had a loft on Broadway at Waverly Place in which he lived and housed a photography studio. He dabbled in dance, photography, and acting. The den mother of the loft was named Sallie and was the most unattractive woman I had ever known. The only job I knew her to have was painting flowers on pottery, which she did in the loft at a penny a plate. Most people have at least one feature on which you can compliment them but not Sallie. She had frizzy hair, little eyes set too close together, a big nose, sloping shoulders, a short waist, and big hips. She was an opera buff and supposedly a lesbian, which made me very uncomfortable at first. I say "supposedly" because on more than one occasion she got lucky and picked up a guy while waiting for standing room at the opera. She always told us about it, saying that she had to keep her options open and it was good to know what you were missing. I lost contact with her but heard that eventually she married, had two kids, moved to Spain for a while, and was now a happy housewife in the Bronx.

We ate a lot of spaghetti, played intellectual, and dressed in a lot of black. If I could have found some, I probably would have had black underwear. Handmade sandals were very stylish that year, but I couldn't afford them. All the talk was of Gide, Proust, and "Froid." Gide was not a problem—I found him in the library, read him, and enjoyed his writing. Proust was a different story. I read *Swann's Way* and understood nothing, but I did manage to learn enough names and events to look like I knew something when the talk was of Proust. I doubted if anyone else had read further than I did. "Froid" was the big problem—either this man was so popular he was always out of circulation, or he was so obscure that even the New York Public Library didn't have him. I'd go to the library and find two shelves of books by someone named Freud, and right after him should have been the man I wanted, Froid, but his books were never on the shelves.

One day I met a girl named Norma at the loft. She was from the Bronx, an artist, and was married and living with her professor husband in Champlain, Illinois. She had a friend named Denny who was one of the group. Denny was a very effeminate guy. Norma said that her family never made any remarks about Denny until one day he came to pick up Norma for an outing. When Norma arrived home, she found her mother crying and asked her what was wrong. Her mother responded that Denny had been wearing a lavender shirt. The cat was finally out of the bag.

Evidently, one night Sallie bedded Norma, and the next day Norma was on a train back to her husband in Illinois. A month later, she was divorcing her husband and was shacking up with a female social worker in Chicago. I kept in contact with Norma for many years, seeing her when I was in Chicago and meeting a couple of her new lovers. She and one of her lovers spent a couple of years in Greece, eating goat cheese and painting. Eventually she moved back to New York, became a Buddhist, lived with a tiny Japanese man, and, I hope, lived happily ever after.

Weekdays were for work and classes. Saturdays were for the theater. Every Saturday I would get up early and get in line for standing room of the latest hit. Only the sold-out hits sold standing room, but there always seemed to be a new show to see. It cost a dollar and a half for matinees and a dollar seventy-five for evenings, which was about the price of the cheapest seats and had a much better view. There was also camaraderie in standing room, and I made several friends there. I saw most of the hits from standing room, and there was little I didn't see if the show lasted a few weeks. I usually had enough money left to take in a movie at one of the Forty-Second Street theaters, which showed the movies as soon as they left the Times Square theaters. The first run theaters cost more — a dollar twenty-five or a dollar and half — so I seldom splurged for them unless they also had a vaudeville bill with someone I wanted to see.

On my first weekend in New York, I saw Beatrice Lilly in *Inside U.S.A.* and took in the New York City Ballet at the City Center. *South Pacific* opened a couple of weeks after I arrived, and I think it took three attempts before I got in line early enough to get standing room tickets. I saw *A Streetcar Named Desire, Death of a Salesman, Lend an Ear* and *Kiss Me Kate*. I fell in love with Julie Harris in *A Member of the Wedding* and *I Am a Camera*. The tickets at Town Hall for the *Town Meeting of the Air* were free so I went frequently. Once I saw Al Capp, of all people, debating Norman Thomas, and I think Capp got the best of Thomas. The wealth of things to see in New York was dizzying for a kid from Brown City. I loved the theaters, the buildings themselves. I loved the ritual and the comfort and the experiences gained within these magical places. I soon had my favorites. For musicals, I liked the 46ᵗʰ Street Theatre; for dramas, I liked the Henry Miller, the Broadhurst, and the National, which was smaller, so if I bought a cheap seat, it was usually in the last couple of rows, and I could see and hear perfectly well. If you sat in the upper reaches of the Broadway or the Majestic, it seemed like you were a block away from the stage. Standing room at the Winter Garden was the worst. "Standees" sat on a bench along the back row of the orchestra floor. You were ten feet behind the last row of the orchestra, which had a glass partition on top of the railing, so "standees" were twice removed from the performance. I avoided standing at the Winter Garden. I made a list of the theaters and checked off which ones I had been in. Eventually I knew all the theaters except the Playhouse, which was torn down before I was able to attend a performance there. I was partial to theaters that were named after the streets they were on. I always thought it was practical to name the theater after the street because it let you know where it was. These were the 46th Street, the 48th Street, and for a while the Adelphi was the 54th Street Theatre. The 44th Street Theatre was gone before I arrived in New York.

I learned to "second act" shows, which entails nonchalantly walking in with the crowd after the intermission. I only did it for musicals and only in summer because in winter there was the problem of having to wear a heavy coat, and I always felt I would be pretty obvious. I saw *Texas, Li'l Darling* five times and never did see the first act.

Sometime during the year, I moved to a rooming house on West Ninety-Fourth Street. And, sometime during that year, I began to realize that modern dance was not what was being used on Broadway. Most of the choreographers were ballet choreographers. Once in a while, someone like Helen Tamiris did a show, but the salable technique was ballet, and I was going to have to learn it. Back to square one, where to start learning ballet? I searched Carnegie Hall and ended up at Ballet Arts because they had classes as late as nine o'clock at night. That meant I could go from Martha Graham's to Carnegie Hall and take a ballet class.

Ballet Arts was on the sixth floor of Carnegie Hall. It was a confusing place because on leaving the elevator on the sixth floor, if you walked down a flight of stairs, you found yourself on the seventh floor. Half a flight to the right was Studio 61, and another half flight put you on the eighth floor. On the door to Studio 61 was the name Ballet Arts along with the names Anton Dolin, Margaret Craske, Edward Caton, Antony Tudor, Lisan Kay, and Agnes de Mille. A sometimes tyrannical and sometimes wonderful woman named Virginia Lee ran the studio. Rumor was that she had married Nimura to give him citizenship, but that he and Miss Kay were lovers. They all seemed to live together in a studio next to Studio 61. Miss Lee had an adopted sixteen-year-old son named Dean Crane whom she was pushing for stardom. He was my first ballet teacher.

I was not aware of it at the time, but I had magically landed in the center of the dance world. Ever since *Oklahoma!*, ballet was "in" on Broadway. Since de Mille's success with *Oklahoma!*, most musicals used ballet choreographers, and Ballet Arts was where all the dancers dutifully came for their daily classes. Starting at eleven in the morning, there were one-and-a-half-hour professional-level classes with various teachers. The last professional-level class started at five-thirty, finishing at seven just in time to get to the theater for the eight o'clock check-in time. There were other studios such as the School of American Ballet at Fifty-Ninth and Madison, and other teachers such as Celli, Tatiana Chamie, and Mme. Anderson, but Ballet Arts was the center of it all, the clearinghouse for rumors and socializing. So, three times a week after my classes at Martha Graham's, I'd jump on the subway and head for Carnegie Hall, not yet aware of what went on there during the day.

The one fly in the ointment of my new life came by mail, an order to report to the Whitehall Induction Center for an Army physical. Being drafted would ruin my dreams. I had a friend who bleached his hair, plucked his eyebrows, and limped his wrists. I didn't have the nerve to do that, but I made sure I pointed my feet when I was asked to jump. When they asked how I felt being in a room with naked men, I replied, "Nervous," which was true because the whole procedure made me nervous.

It worked—they called me a 5A. I didn't understand exactly what that meant except that I wasn't going into the Army unless there was a very dire emergency.

# * Chapter 3 *

_M_ ost of the evening classes, whether ballet or modern dance, were beginners' classes for either aspiring young people who had day jobs or for dilettantes who wanted to exercise and to keep a foot in the door. In order to partake of the day activities, I had a little rearranging to do. I needed a night job. The job I found was as the night manager at a Hanson's Bakery on Avenue B and Fourteenth Street, working from five to eleven. It paid less than thirty dollars per week, but I could guarantee myself a free meal of bread and cake from the stale stuff that hadn't been sold.

I found the job through a friend, Dale, who I had met at the Martha Graham studio. Dale was a mediocre dancer but was probably a genius. He and his lover had both been in the road company of _Brigadoon,_ so I thought I was running in pretty hot company. Some might brag that they've had a postcard from George Bernard Shaw, but Dale had _letters_ from him. Dale became my mentor. After work at the bakery, I would go to their place and talk the night away. He was always good at explaining what Martha had said or had been referring to in class that day. He was a great admirer of Eugene O'Neill, and through correspondence had ingratiated himself with O'Neill's wife, Carlotta. A few years later, I had to exchange my opening night tickets to Judy Garland at the Palace for second night tickets because Dale had secured rights to and was doing a dance/mime version of *Mourning Becomes Electra* on Judy's opening night. That was loyalty! Years later, Dale's leading dancer, who had gone to Europe and joined the Marquis de Cuevas dance company, was stabbed to death by his lover who didn't want him to leave on tour.

Working at night allowed me to take the intermediate classes at Graham's and the more advanced beginner and intermediate classes at Ballet Arts. The world of ballet was exploding and was pulling at me. The Sadler's Wells Ballet with Margot Fonteyn had conquered New York. Ballet Theatre and New York City Ballet were having successful seasons. The Russians were coming. Ballet was popular. Fate had been kind by leading me into it.

I auditioned for a modern dance concert and was accepted. The choreography was done by a Lillian Shapiro. I ran around the Washington Irving High School Auditorium shouting *mazel tov*, having no idea what it meant, but she paid me fifteen dollars, my first dance wages. I immediately bought a pair of handmade sandals in the Village. Sandals were very popular with the beatniks. I never wore them much because they embarrassed me when I was uptown, and I seemed to gravitate towards uptown because that's where things seemed to be happening more than in the Village.

Monday afternoons at the Museum of Modern Art were a must because they showed old movies with Gloria Swanson, Greta Garbo, John Gilbert, and lots of foreign movies which were popular such as the British comedies with Alec Guinness.

Up early, I would go to Ballet Arts for my ballet class then would spend the day watching the advanced and professional classes until it was time to go to the Village for my Martha Graham class. I sat by the door of the studio watching thirty to forty students take Margaret Craske's class and when that was over, I watched another thirty or forty students take Edward Caton's class, and then Anthony Tudor's class. It was exciting.

These were professional working dancers who were in all the current hit shows. I listened to all the gossip and knew who was in what show, what shows were about to cast, and who had hopes for this or that show. I heard which shows were "in trouble" out of town, which ones were supposed to be hits, and which choreographers were about to be fired. It was pretty close to being in the theater.

With trepidation, I sneaked into the advanced class. Miss Lee was very strict about who was and who was not ready to advance. I never knew her to tell anyone that they were ready to advance, but if you sneaked in and she didn't yank you out, it was understood that you'd be welcome to stay at the new level. She didn't yank me out.

Classes had an unspoken etiquette. Professionals chose where they wanted to work at the barre and in the center. The advanced students came next then the least adept took up the less desirable places. In the center of the studio, professionals went in the first group and up front unless they chose to go to the rear or with the second group. Women took precedence over the men unless a man was a really big star. If one presumed to go front and center, one risked great embarrassment by being told to go to the second group or to the rear. The tacit idea was that one learned from the "pros," an idea that seems to have been lost in our egalitarian society. Nowadays, placement in class is a free-for-all.

Bonnie Mendelsohn asked me to be her partner. Bonnie was "left wing" as was most of the modern dance world. That was fine by me because it would shock Mom. I was not adverse to shocking the family to show them how sophisticated I had become. It never worked—she refused to be shocked, or at least to show it. Bonnie and I dyed pants and tee shirts for costumes, and she did the choreography. We participated in a few concerts at various venues including the YMCA and the Jefferson School.

About this time, I changed my name. When one went into the theater, after all, didn't one change one's name? "Tuttle" when pronounced with the New York glottal stop became Tuddle or Tut'll, and I didn't like it. I chose "Gavin," straight out of A.J. Cronin's *The Green Years*. Lisan Kay, one of my ballet teachers, said it was fine numerologically. I was inching towards "show biz" with a new name and even making a few extra dollars with concerts.

The grapevine was beginning to work. One day I received a telegram from Sophie Maslow asking me to join the New Dance Group for a tour. It had been formed by Sophie, Jane Dudley, and William Bales. It was very proletarian. Jane and Sophie had been Graham dancers. Bales, married to Jo Van Vleet, had been part of Humphrey's group. Each of them contributed to the repertory that mostly contained dances commenting on social, political, and Jewish themes.

In one number, I was cast as a rabbi. Me! In Brown City, we had eight churches but no synagogue. In Flint, I knew a friend who went to synagogue instead of church and missed some days at school. That was all I knew about Jewish culture, although a good proportion of my new friends were Jewish. I was always a little self-conscious about religion, coming from a nonreligious family. Whenever I went into a church, I was afraid the roof would collapse, and when the dust cleared everyone would be staring at me with scorn. Anyway, a rabbi I was. I also had the unenviable position of replacing Ronnie Aul, who had had tremendous critical and popular success in Sophie's *The Village I Knew*.

When rehearsals ended, I gave up my job and my room, and we were off on a two-week tour. We played mostly colleges, but we did have an engagement at The Detroit Art Institute, sixty miles from Flint, which enabled Mom and my sister, Mary, to see me dance. I had the distinct impression that they were not too impressed. But what did they know about modern dance? What did I know? In New York, most modern dance concerts were held at the YMHA or Hunter College. Most tours were to colleges and universities that had modern dance courses. Modern dance had entered the universities, but very few of them had ballet courses. Only Martha Graham had the name and the financial backing to be booked into the regular commercial theaters. In pre-NEA (National Endowment for the Arts) and Ford Foundation days, artists had to scrounge for money from wealthy backers from the private sector. Martha Graham had the likes of the Harkness family and Katherine Cornell who would occasionally back her.

This tour was the beginning of having to change my residence every time I had a job. I could never afford to keep my room while I was out of town, but finding a room was never any problem. The West Side was full of single occupancy brownstones, so an afternoon patrolling the streets always produced a new place to stay. I think that at one time or another, I've lived on all the blocks between Sixty-Third and Ninety-Sixth Streets. At one time I lived where the promenade of the New York State Theater at Lincoln Center currently is. In those days, it was a rough Puerto Rican neighborhood called San Juan Hill. It was razed in the 1960s to become Lincoln Center. Another time, a girl and I rented an art gallery in the Village that was closed for the summer. It was very Bohemian with a kitchen and two sleeping lofts accessed by ladders behind the gallery walls. It was very romantic until you had to climb down that ladder in the dark to use the john. We were there only a few weeks when there was a knock at the door. When we answered were presented with a subpoena addressed to Jane and Mary Doe. It stated that we were illegal tenants. I didn't mind being kicked out, but I did think we could have been addressed as Jane and John Doe. Expelled from the gallery, we moved into Mark Ryder's and Emily Frankel's rehearsal studio while they were on tour. This too was illegal, so we lived in fear that the fire department would find that we were there. All cooking utensils and hot plates had to be hidden during the day in case there was a surprise inspection.

After the New Dance Group tour, I ended up at my favorite

New York residence, a room on the parlor floor of 11 Bank Street facing the end of Waverly Place. The landlords lived in the basement and had a baby girl named Starr, which I thought was a dumb name for a kid. Years later, she and her mother turned up at a stage door as balletomanes, and later the girl became a principal dancer with the Joffrey Ballet.

I got a new job as an usher at Radio City Music Hall. Same pay—all my jobs paid the same—but what glamour! Working at the Music Hall was almost like being in show business. We had two tailored uniforms, one for the day shift and one for the night shift. Everyday before going on to the floor we had inspection to make sure our shirt collars and white gloves were clean, our bow ties straight, our shoes shined, and our flashlights in working order. After inspection, we were marched to the floor and given our assignments for the day. We were assigned specific aisles, floors, and doors. The plum assignment was the first mezzanine that was reserved seating. If you advanced and were assigned to the elevators, you earned two dollars more per week and sometimes relieved the backstage elevator operator which afforded contact with the Rockettes.

Radio City Music Hall was the premier movie theater in New York. Films that premiered there advertised themselves as having opened at the Music Hall. It was sheer prestige. Audiences lined up outside for hours before the first show. On Christmas or Easter or for a very popular movie, the lines would go around the block. Amazingly, the crowds took it all in good spirit, as an adventure, and there were seldom problems controlling the crowds.

Working the first mezzanine also allowed you to see celebrities who entered through the Executive Entrance and were brought to the first mezzanine by private elevator. And, of course, there was a chance to get a tip. Tipping was not officially allowed, and the uniforms had no pockets, so there was the problem of where to keep the quarters that were offered. A few could be stuffed into the fingers of the white gloves and, on a good day, the shoes could be used or, as a last resort, the cummerbund could be stuffed, but the quarters tended to fall out. On a really good night, you could make a couple of extra dollars, but a dollar was generally considered a boon. One night, the manager brought the Duchess of Windsor to my aisle. As I took her to a seat and handed her a program, she stealthily slipped a folded dollar into my palm. She was so smooth that I hardly realized it had happened. I have thought well of the Duchess ever since.

"Stripping" was the headache of the first mezzanine. The reserved seats were sold twice a day, once for the matinee and once for the evening show. If the holder of the matinee seat did not come for that first show, that seat was empty until the evening show. The theater sold unmarked tickets and we put those patrons in empty seats. Unfortunately, patrons for the evening show might come early, so we'd put them in nearby seats whose ticket holders might arrive next. It became a big juggling act, trying to remember who was in what seat and when they might be leaving. I remember only a few times when the manager had to be called to smooth talk someone and straighten out a sticky situation.

One night I was told to go up to the conference room where there was to be a reception for General Eisenhower. I went up and was assigned to his hat. When the General arrived, he gave his hat to an aide who handed the hat to me. They went into the reception, and I was instructed to hold the hat with two hands. It was not to be put on a shelf or a table. It was to remain in my hands until the reception was over. Afterwards, the aide took the hat, handed it to the General, and they left. I'm not sure they even noticed me. The General was no Duchess. And, yes, I tried on the hat.

During the last show, there was not much to do except stand around and direct people to the restrooms and the exits. I used to stand in front of the mirrors at the top of the staircase trying to wiggle my ears. I had seen some character in a movie do it. I practiced to no avail until one night they started to move and I couldn't stop them. I had visions of going through life with twitching ears. I can still do it and am a great success when flirting with children on the subway.

After the last show, we did the "search." We checked all the rows looking for lost articles. You wouldn't believe all the lost gloves we'd find in one night. Small change we could keep, but wallets and any money in them were to be turned in. One night my moral fiber was put to the test and it lost. I found a wallet with thirty-five dollars in it, more than a week's pay. I turned in the wallet but kept the money, and the next day went to Robert Hall, a discount men's clothing store, to buy a new suit for Easter. I wore it on Easter Sunday with such guilt that it took me months before I would put it on again. In its lifetime, I didn't wear it more than three times, always with the guilt baggage.

The Music Hall provided jobs to a lot of aspiring theater people. George Maharis worked as an usher for a time while I was there. We saw a lot of great movies. I watched *American in Paris* and *Singing in the Rain* for seven weeks, seldom missing the musical numbers.

The world of ballet was growing fast and new schools were opening. Ballet Theatre opened a school and took Edward Caton from Ballet Arts. Margaret Craske and Anthony Tudor left to open a school at the Metropolitan Opera. Vladimir Dokoudovsky, Nina Stroganova, Nana Goldner, and Paul Petroff started teaching. Goldner was a ballerina with Ballet Theatre and always taught in street clothes. It was a sight to see her demonstrate jumps in high heels. She supposedly had fines for arriving late to the theater built into her contract. She also had favorite shoes for particular steps and spent a lot of time in the wings changing shoes. She was married to Petroff, who had been with Ballet Russe and had a reputation as a "ladies man." During one of the Ballet Russe's annual Christmas engagements in Chicago, he was stabbed. He never told who did it, but his roles mysteriously improved after the incident.

Dokoudovsky and Stroganova were a married couple who had been with Colonel de Basil's Ballet Russe. They were on a South American tour when World War II broke out and were unable to return home, so they toured South America for five years. Stroganova was a gentle Danish woman who gave a deceptively difficult class. I loved to hear her count—one, two, twee—and one time she berated me for yawning, considering it a sign of boredom. I thought that it was a compliment to come to class even though I was tired, but I never yawned in her class again.

Dokoudovsky was spectacular. He had just retired from performing, was young enough to be very physical, and he enjoyed showing off. Demonstrating a combination, he would soar across the studio in one jump, and all combinations would end with his doing eighteen to twenty pirouettes. Only Jacques D'Amboise could compete with him. For my money, he gave the best class I ever took. Perhaps he wasn't the best teacher but his classes were complete and his students had the chance to work on complete techniques. I took his class for more than four years and never could understand him because of his accent. He spoke about eight languages, and I wondered if he spoke all of them with an accent, including Russian.

I continued to take classes at Martha Graham's but my focus was more and more on ballet. There was a time when Graham needed a new male dancer for her company. My hopes were up. Everyone was telling me that I was the logical one for her to choose but she didn't. She went to the American School of Ballet and hired someone from there. It was a big disappointment, but, in a way, I understood. Graham was so powerful that she always had "big" men around her and I was not "big."

Life was exciting. I rubbed shoulders with the famous and revelled in the romance of the teachers. When Roland Petit's company came to New York, I could watch and compare Petit, Jeanmaire, Colette Marchand, Leslie Caron, Lilliane Montevechi, and George Zorich in class. The club acts like

Giselle & Francois Szony, and Augie & Margo were in class.
Even Butterfly McQueen turned up from time to time. After
Kovachs and Rabovsky "jumped over the wall" from Hungary,
they came to class. I could evaluate myself against the working
New York dancers. I was improving, and my dreams were
not too far-fetched. The teachers were demanding but kind,
although sometimes you had to decipher that the kindness and
concern were buried behind gruff exteriors. One day, Paul
Petroff arrived late to Edward Caton's class. Caton said, "Paul,
you're late. Where have you been?"

Paul, irritated, replied, "I was fucking."

And Caton said, "Well, at least you were doing something
constructive—two, three, four."

Agnes de Mille was frequently in class, standing at the
center barre. Agnes wasn't pretending to compete in class. She
was there for conditioning and usually left as the jumps began.
She had the prettiest feet and calves, small and well developed.
However, above the knees, she had begun to blossom. The
seams of her tights wound around her legs above the knees,
giving her a rather disheveled look.

I started going to auditions for shows. I didn't get too far
at first. All shows had three auditions. The first was for Actors'
Equity members only, the second an "open" call, and then a
final call was for those who had made the cut of the first two.
Very few people were chosen from the open call, but there was
always "that chance." If you succeeded and you got a show, you
had to join the union and got to receive your Equity Card, and
then you could go to the Equity calls. Possessing an Equity card
was critically important. Without one, you couldn't go very far.

One time I got close in an audition for a replacement for
*Guys and Dolls*. Auditions for replacements were usually open
calls, and I was kept at this one until there were only six dancers
left. Michael Kidd, the choreographer, came down the line
saying something to each of us, making his final selection. He
got to me, looked at me, and said, "I think you're too young."

There were lots of stories about auditioning at the Equity call, not getting the job, changing your clothes, going to the open call, and getting the job. So, when a few weeks later, there was another open call for a replacement in *Guys and Dolls*, I dressed in different clothes and went to the audition. Again, I was kept until there were six of us. Michael came walking down the line. When he got to me, he looked at me and said, "You're still too young."

There seemed to be a progression in auditioning. First you get eliminated early, then you last a while, then you almost get picked, and after a while, you always get picked. Then you start the whole process over in the final audition. In the meantime, your technique improves, and you learn to dress and present yourself, but it is still a demeaning, nerve-wracking experience.

I finally got my Equity card through a job with a stock company at the Court Square Theater in Springfield, Massachusetts, where I spent Christmas 1951 and earned seventy-five dollars a week. We did two shows, *The Merry Widow* and *Finian's Rainbow*.

I've done two productions of *Finian's*, and in both the leading lady insisted on singing, "When the idle rich become the idle poor..." which she started to realize was wrong when the next line, "You'll never know just who is who or who is which..." wouldn't rhyme. It gave a rather capitalistic bent to the socialistic direction of the book.

At least we were in a regular theater for this engagement. I heard of one production of *Finian's* done in the round, and when the actor playing a senator who is turned into a black man ran up the aisle during a blackout to have his face painted black, he was preceded by a member of the audience who had importunely decided to use the john at that moment. I never heard whether the audience member made it to the john, but he did get his face blackened.

In the late spring of 1952, I finally broke through. I auditioned for Daniel Nagrin and got a job working at Green

Mansions for the summer. For the next eighteen years, I earned my living as a dancer. There was to be no more usher, bakery clerk, or "sortographer" on my resume.

# * Chapter 4 *

D aniel Nagrin was a modern dancer as well as the husband of Helen Tamiris. He had had success doing revues on Broadway and was branching out as a choreographer. In one of those strange twists of fate that you know are meaningful without knowing exactly how, Nagrin dropped out as choreographer to do a movie, *His Majesty O'Keefe*, with Burt Lancaster. Rod Alexander and Bambi Linn were signed to replace him as choreographers.

Green Mansions wasn't a summer stock operation. It didn't do revivals of musical shows. It was a hybrid theater workshop started by Lena Barish and Sam Garlen. It funded itself through a resort patronized mostly by young Jews on vacation looking for mates. It provided rustic accommodations, a dining hall, a lake with rowboats and canoes, tennis courts, and a small theater for the nightly entertainment. There might be a chamber concert, a play, an abbreviated opera, or at the end of the week, a musical revue. It was near Warrensburg in the Adirondack Mountains. It was similar to Tamiment, which was also famous as an incubator of talent in the Poconos. The performers were given rooms in cabins on the other side of the lake, board, plus a small salary of thirty-five dollars a week.

The performers were young and unknown, but several have since had success of varying degrees. Michael Ross and Bernie

West of *All in the Family* fame were the producer and comedian. Faith Dane, the trumpet playing stripper in *Gypsy*, was a featured performer. Charles Strouse was the rehearsal pianist who even then was talking of a musical version of *Orphan Annie*, although first he was to succeed with *Bye Bye Birdie*, which he wrote with Lee Adams. The leading lady was a Green Mansions' version of Carol Burnett. She could sing and was a wonderful comedienne. She had had a couple of supporting roles on Broadway and was considered a "comer." Unfortunately, her career came to a grinding halt a couple of years later when she stabbed her husband to death during a domestic hassle.

Rod was stuck with the dancers that Nagrin had hired before he left, and a disparate group were we. There were six of us, three men and three women. One man and one woman were very tall. The rest of us were of moderate size. The women were basically modern dancers and the men were more ballet oriented. The tall woman was the wonderful Felisa Conde. She was Charles Weidman's leading dancer. She was married to a dancer, Nick Vanoff, who later became a television producer. Felisa had a beautiful technique, and in a few years, she became a choreographer in her own right, doing the *Steven Allen Show*, the *Perry Como Show* and the Kennedy Center honors show on television.

Bambi Linn, who was as sweet as her name, had been in *Oklahoma!* and then played the daughter in *Carousel*, after which she played "Alice" in Evan LaGallienne's, *Alice in Wonderland*. She was star quality and one of the loves of my life.

Rod Alexander had been part of Jack Cole's group and did a lot of the Forties movie musicals. He had a baby face, was strong as an ox, and had the most stretched Achilles tendons I had ever seen. He could stand on one leg and lower himself to the floor on his knee using no hands. He was strange and moody, and he became one of the loves of my life. I adored both of them. They had met and married while performing in a musical show and had created a very successful club act doing spectacular lifts that equaled or outdid the Ballet Russe. They did lifts that were based on the peculiar proportions of their bodies, and no one else could do them. They had others that were strictly timing and if missed, Bambi would end up flat on the floor on her face. There was no recovery and no room for error. They were sensational. They had signed on for the next season as the dance team on Sid Caesar's *Your Show of Shows*. They had taken the Green Mansions job primarily so that they could work on routines and numbers for the coming season.

It was a summer of aching muscles and bleeding feet and terrible tensions. Rod was concentrated and moody. Most choreographers seem to take on the personality traits of their mentors and Rod was straight out of the Jack Cole school. Rod and Bambi told of working for Jack on one number that was so fast that the company had to strain to keep up with the music. One night during performance, the company outdid themselves and finished right on the music. Jack finished two bars later and complained that the company was ahead of the music. Rod tended to be like that too. He was very demanding. "Good" or "very good" received no compliments, only the expectation of better.

We rehearsed three weeks' worth of programs so that guests who stayed more than one week did not see the same entertainment repeated. We kept rehearsing and adding and changing things until the very last day. Rod was tough, but he managed to do a number featuring each of the dancers. In his own way, he was very solicitous of us. He and Bambi worked on their spectacular numbers. One night at dinner, Felisa, who had been suffering from a toothache and had had no time to go to a dentist, broke down in tears. Sobbing, she said "If only it would stop for five minutes, I could bear the pain some more." I think she finally got time to go to the dentist.

During the last week, we finally had a day off, and I hitched a ride to New York. It was great timing since there was an audition for a show I especially wanted to do. Bette Davis was going to do a Jerome Robbins revue called *Two's Company*. Robbins was the premier choreographer of the day, and if he was doing a show it was probably going to be a hit. The next best bet would be Michael Kidd. Oh, to be in a show with my favorite actress and to work for Robbins! Everyone wanted to work for Robbins despite the horror tales that abounded about working with him. He was the best, and it gave you an extra cachet to be known as a Robbins dancer.

I went to the audition, and at the end, a group of names were called to stay. The rest were to leave. I thought but wasn't sure that my name was called, so I approached Robbins to ask if I had heard my name. He studied me for a moment then said, "No, I think not." The way he said it made me think I had been right, but my question had given him the chance to change his mind. Or, maybe, he didn't want any deaf dancers. Bette and I were not to be.

So, back to Green Mansions for the final week of performances, then to pack up my things, find a new place to live in New York, sign up for unemployment insurance, and start classes again. I snuck into Dokoudovsky's professional class, and Virginia Lee did not kick me out. I hadn't matched Neil Armstrong who would make a giant leap for mankind on the moon some years later, but I'd taken a few steps forward in my career—I'd had three solid months of employment as a dancer.

There was one darkening cloud on the horizon, however. During the summer, I had noticed that my comb had an awful lot of hair in it. Another of the dancers had thinning hair and spent hours a day with a vibrator applied to his scalp. When I arrived back in New York, I purchased my first vibrator.

# * Chapter 5 *

S ettled once again in New York, I auditioned for a small ballet company that was being formed. I went to the audition more for experience than in expectation of a job. I didn't think my ballet technique was good enough for a company, but as Agnes de Mille said in one of her books, "You offer yourself, let others judge." I was selected to join the Slavenska-Franklin Ballet company as a dancer, and shortly thereafter I was made the assistant stage manager. The company manager and stage manager was Kurt Newman, Mia Slavenska's husband. Kurt was Hungarian. His first wife had been a member of the Communist party, and—this being the McCarthy era of the Fifties—he was on a secret list, so he could not leave the country for fear that he would not be allowed back in. When we went to Canada, Kurt had to stay in the States, so it was up to me to supervise the stage crew. Fortunately for me they knew their jobs and needed little supervision from me. I could give lighting and curtain cues with a nod of my head while I was onstage dancing.

Mia Slavenska was a Yugoslavian ballerina who had danced with the Ballet Russe in Europe, had won an Olympic medal, and had starred in the French movie, *Ballerina*. She was a handsome, red-headed woman with a fabulous technique and extraordinary balances. She also had the idiosyncratic reputation of dancing without ribbons on her toe shoes. She once told me that she had never danced with ribbons but had publicity photographs taken with them only to make her legs look longer. Her legs were a little short. For several years, Mia had toured with a small concert company, Ballet Variante, which she had formed under the aegis of Columbia Concerts. This concert group was to be the nucleus of the new company.

Mia did not like to dance *Swan Lake*. One night I was standing in the wings with Ronnie Colton when she came off stage from doing *Swan Lake*. She said, "I've never danced so badly in my life."

Ronnie said, "Oh no, Mia, I've seen you worse." Mia looked at him, gave a clawlike movement with her hand and laughed. She did not take herself too seriously.

Frederic Franklin was an Englishman who had started dancing in the English music halls before joining the Ballet Russe. He was an exceptional partner and an engaging performer. He told me that when World War II started, the company had been rehearsing in Monte Carlo and were due to leave for Paris. Not knowing what to do, the company dutifully gathered at the Monte Carlo train station, and when the train, which had started in Menton, arrived, it did not stop. The train pulled slowly through the station. Standing on the observation platform was the company ballet master, Jean Yasinski, yelling, "Rehearsals in Paris on Tuesday." Somehow the company managed to get to Paris. Frederic spent the next ten years partnering with Alexandra Danilova on tours across the contiguous forty-eight states. Fred said that when he first joined the company, Danilova treated him as a young brother, then as an equal, and then as an older brother.

Mia and Fred had joined forces to create the Slavenska-Franklin Ballet, a company of twenty-two dancers including the guest star, Alexandra Danilova. The basic program was to be *Swan Lake*, *A Streetcar Named Desire*, *Madamoiselle Fifi*, and *The Nutcracker*. We also did a Cesar Franck ballet and the *pas de deux* from *Don Quixote* to give variation to the program. Slavenska and Danilova shared the roles in *Swan Lake* and *The Nutcracker. Streetcar* was a showcase for Slavenska, and *Fifi* was a trifle to show off Danilova. Mixing the ballets up, we had two different programs.

Alexandra Danilova, *guest artiste* with the company, was probably America's most famous and adored ballerina. Born in St. Petersburg, she left Russia with Balanchine and danced with Diaghilev's Ballet Russe and various permutations of the Ballet Russe. She ended up in America as prima ballerina for the Denham Ballet Russe de Monte Carlo, where she toured the country introducing ballet to America. She was Balanchine's second wife, although there is some question as to whether they were married, and if they had been, whether they had ever bothered with a divorce. She was a grand and kind lady who would help the new girls with their makeup. At receptions, she would present her cheek to me to be kissed, a ritual I began to realize was not homage to her but rather one to raise me in the esteem of whomever was present. If we met each other with no one important around, we shook hands. After her retirement from dancing, she spent years teaching at the American School of Ballet. I had tears in my eyes watching her receive the Kennedy Center Honors for the Performing Arts in 1989.

Slavenska commissioned Valerie Bettis to do the choreography of *Streetcar* to an arrangement of Alex North's music from the movie version. Peter Larkin designed an atmospheric set. As a ballet, it was probably small potatoes, but as a theatrical piece it was quite impressive, providing Slavenska as Blanche, Franklin as Stanley, and Lois Ellyn as Stella, with wonderful roles in which they all had enormous success.

During rehearsals, I had an embarrassing episode with knitting. At this time, before Danskin tights were invented, one had three choices for tights—silk, an expensive choice; cotton, which bagged at the knees the first time it was worn; or store bought wool, which was itchy. The only way to obtain soft wool tights was to make them. I bought some wool and knitting needles. Someone taught me to cast on stitches then how to knit and purl. I went home that night, cast on, knit a row, and came out with too many stitches. I worked for hours to get it right, and when I did, I knitted until dawn. My forearms were so sore that tears came to my eyes when I touched my arms. I had to go to rehearsal and lift Slavenska. It hurt like hell, but I was not about to tell anyone I had sprained my arms knitting.

Rehearsals finished and we went to Quebec to open the production. For the next eight months we spent a good part of our lives on a bus. We were one of the first "bus and truck" operations, which meant that the cast traveled by bus and the sets traveled by truck, while the crew and orchestra conductor went by car. As soon as a performance was finished, the set was struck and loaded into the truck. The set and the car with the crew headed for the next stop. The cast headed for the hotel and, in the morning got on the bus for that day's journey. Whether we traveled a hundred miles or three hundred miles to the next engagement, the bus trip always seemed to last eight hours. If the bus stopped at a crossroads with four service stations for a rest stop, everyone lined up at the same one. Lunch stops became longer if the miles to be traveled were less. While the cast traveled, the crew put up the set at the next theater, and the conductor rehearsed the pick-up orchestra in the next city. The cast usually arrived late in the afternoon in time to check into a hotel, have something to eat, go to the theater, and warm up to start all over again. It was mostly one night stands except for weekends when we usually played for two days in larger cities.

On the bus, Mia had the two front seats on the passenger side, and Fred had the two seats right behind her. Danilova had the two front seats on the left side, and her dresser, Elizabeth Twisdom, had the seat behind her. As assistant stage manager, I shared a seat with Lois Ellyn. The rest of the company, including a couple of lead musicians and the wardrobe mistress, filled the other seats. The bus driver was a tyrant. We probably treated him as a cipher, dropping our bags at the side of the bus for him to load, but he was not about to be ignored. When he said, "March," we marched. If someone requested a rest stop, we had to wait until he decided it was time, but he always got us to the next show on time.

A good portion of the time on the bus we slept, read, wrote letters and did crossword puzzles. If your seat was near the heating units, it was too hot, and if not, it was too cold. I spent a lot of my time knitting, my forearms being strong enough by this time. I made tights for myself then started making them as presents for others. Lois spent her time darning her toe shoes. Sometimes, when she was displeased with someone, she would draw their faces on her shoes before she darned over them so she could dance on their faces.

I stayed in the YMCA at a dollar twenty-five per night. I acquired a great collection of towels. Most of the company stayed in hotels using a money saving procedure called "ghosting." One person would register then another would share the room surreptitiously. Once I saw a company member playing the role of ghost to the hilt. He was flitting from post to post on his way across the lobby to the elevator hoping he wouldn't be seen. The hotel managements were probably aware of the situation but seldom made a fuss.

Just before Christmas, we had a New York engagement of two weeks before a two-week break. I was finally about to work in a real New York theater, the Century, at 932 Seventh Avenue between Fifty-Eighth Street and Central Park South. It was the theater furthest north of the legitimate theaters closer to Times Square, but it was a genuine New York theater and I was thrilled. On opening night, I finally heard "it."

For our opening in New York, Danilova was scheduled to appear in *The Nutcracker* as the closing ballet of the evening. She had not appeared in New York for the several years since she had left Ballet Russe. When the curtain went up on *The Nutcracker*, she was sitting on Roland Vazques's shoulder. Suddenly the noise of applause and cheers hit like a thunderclap, enough to knock you over. For the next three or four minutes, you could not hear the music. It was a special sound of excitement, of love, and of appreciation for what has been and what will be. Once you've heard it, you have no doubt about wanting to be in the theater.

We received good reviews and were extended for an extra week. After the Christmas break, we were back on the bus heading to Pittsburgh. Then, in twenty-eight days, we toured back to the East Coast, turned South, and then West and ended up in Tucson. That was a lot of knitting, darning toe shoes, eating hamburgers, packing, unpacking, warming up, nursing sprained muscles, and using my new vibrator on my scalp.

Touring, especially one night stands, is rough. Cliques form and re-form. Arguments blaze and fade. Memories blur and sometimes, leaving the theater, you forget what city you're in. You never knew what condition a theater would be in when you arrived. Some theaters were old movie houses with dirty, oily floors that soiled your costumes. Some had drafty dressing rooms that hadn't been cleaned in years with rusty water running in the taps. Occasionally, we'd be in a high school auditorium so the dressing room might be the history classroom. Once in a while, there would be an old gem of a theater like the one we found in Hutchinson, Kansas, with a stage raked in the European style. Dancing on an incline can, however, cause problems when you're not used to it. Pirouettes have to be adjusted. You feel like you're soaring when you leap downstage, but when you leap upstage, the floor comes at you very quickly, jarring the fillings in your teeth. The only other theater in the United States that I know of with a raked stage is the Philadelphia Academy of Music.

One night in Harrisburg, a new member of the company was given a new solo. The company stood in the wings to see how he did. He stepped out onto the stage, posed, took two steps and fell flat on his back. The next night he stepped out, posed, took two steps, and fell flat on his face. During a *ballet blanc*, another dancer slipped and fell. Her vocalized "shit" carried throughout the auditorium. It turned out that the management, trying to do the best for us, had waxed and polished the floor. It shone like a Hollywood set, but it was difficult to remain upright walking across the floor, much less dancing on toe. We mopped the stage with Coca-Cola, which sometimes alleviated slipperiness, but to no avail. That night the girls danced in ballet slippers instead of toe shoes, and there were lots of falling swans. Slavenska and Danilova carefully danced on toe and somehow remained upright with the help of their partners.

One member of the company couldn't wake up in the morning no matter how many alarms he used and, frequently, was absent when it was time for the bus to leave. Sometimes the street was full of dancers, including Slavenska and Danilova, knocking on the doors of rooming houses trying find him. One morning, his sleepy head poked out from a hotel window, and he yelled, "Go on without me!" We went and somehow he made the evening performance.

Jamie Bauer, a beautiful light-skinned Creole ballerina, lived in fear of a racial incident occurring when we toured in the South. There never was one, but Jamie moved to Paris as soon as the tour was over. With Jamie, we played the Daughters of the American Revolution auditorium in Washington, D.C., where Marian Anderson had been forbidden to sing. Jamie was allowed to perform, but down the street, the National Theater was closed because Actor's Equity was boycotting segregated theaters. It was hard to believe that even as late as the 1950s such things existed, especially in the nation's capital. Many of the Southern theaters were segregated, but since the South was not a big theatrical market, not much was made of segregation until Equity took a stand. I wish I could say that it upset me more than it did. Of course, I didn't approve but it was the way things were, and I was not a social activist. I saw my first "Colored Only" and "White Only" signs along the Mason-Dixon line. They made me feel uncomfortable, as though I were in a foreign country. It was a different way of doing things. However, further South of the Mason-Dixon line, those signs were less evident. The races had made their uneasy accommodation to each other. Race was and is a problem in the ballet world. Aesthetic ideas and the desire for uniformity come smack up against the ideals of assimilation.

While we were in Washington, I went to my first embassy reception at the Yugoslavian Embassy. I had read somewhere that Mrs. Roosevelt had said that the Yugoslavians were the best hosts in Washington. This party was the proof of the pudding. It was very grand. I learned to be careful of slivovitz, that strong plum brandy for which the Yugoslavians were known. One of the reasons for the party, other than Slavenska being Yugoslavian, was that there was talk of taking the company to Yugoslavia as the core of a national company, an enterprise that, unfortunately, never happened.

Lee Becker Theodore was in the company. She later created the role of "Anybodys" in *West Side Story*, did the choreography for several shows, and then created The American Dance Machine. Sally Streets was also a member of the company. She later joined the New York City Ballet, got married, and gave us Kyra Nichols. Others from the company have opened schools in various cities across the country.

On one overnight trip during an ice storm, I was sharing a seat with a woman who was married to another company member. She sat in the window seat next to me because she had just had an argument with her husband. In the middle of the night, I awoke to find her crying. Thinking that it was a husband issue, I asked her what the problem was. Did she want to talk about it? She replied, "It's so hot, I can't stand it in here!" There was a foot of snow on the highway, the windows were iced, but you could have fried an egg on the inside of the bus. A few minutes later, we were all jostled awake. We were in a ditch, but the tyrant bus driver got us out, and we arrived at the next engagement on time.

Sometimes the house was full, but sometimes it seemed as though there were more of us on stage than people in the audience. Rumors started floating that the company was going to Japan. We were booked for an entire week into the Geary Theater in San Francisco, usually a good ballet town. We lost our shirts. We played a weekend in Los Angeles, usually not a good ballet town, and sold out every night. We could have played for two weeks. The rumor about going to Japan was verified, but only part of the company was going. I thought my chances of being included were nil, but was informed that I was included. I went to the Japanese consulate to apply for a visa. I had to get shots. I learned that one thing you never want to do is lift a ballerina after a tetanus shot.

We played San Diego where my oldest brother, Freeman, a naval officer, lived with his family. Freeman disapproved of my chosen profession, but I brought him backstage, and he watched one of the ballets from the wings. Danilova flirted with him outrageously—he looked very handsome in his Navy uniform. When he saw how hard the dancers worked, he gained new respect for us. The work ethic was deeply ingrained in him. His wife told me that he said, "Gee, they work so hard."

Leaving San Diego early on a Sunday, we had the worst trip I had ever made. We were to be in Albuquerque Monday night—a long trip. Everything was fine until we passed through Yuma, Arizona where we saw our scenery truck parked at a truck stop. It had left San Diego after the show Saturday night. We stopped to investigate, only to discover that the truck had broken down. It was decided that Kurt Neuman, the company manager, and I would stay in Yuma to arrange for a new truck while the company traveled on to Albuquerque.

Negotiations for a new truck were sticky. The available truckers quickly surmised that we were desperate and had a timing issue. So of course the price went up. Eventually, with a new truck and driver, we left Yuma late in the day with just enough time to get to Albuquerque. The cab of the truck had two seats, one for the driver and one for Kurt. My place was on the hump with the gear shift between the seats. Every time the driver shifted gears, I got hit in the back. I was so cramped that I could not find a position in which one leg or the other did not go to sleep. Kurt was a big man, so there was no way that we could exchange places.

After a couple of hours on the road, we suddenly became aware that we were sitting on a fire. Flames were licking at our derrieres. We pulled to the side of the road to put out the fire, and after inspection, found that nothing was seriously damaged. Back into the cab and on to Albuquerque we went. We drove all night and by the late afternoon of the next day, we were all falling asleep. Fortunately, one or the other of us would wake in time to see that we were about to go off the road. We'd poke the driver awake; he'd align the truck to the road, and we'd feel our eyelids start to droop again. We pulled up to the theater in Albuquerque at eight-thirty, curtain time. The local crew was waiting for us. Somehow they hung the sets, and we started the show at nine, only a half hour late.

We worked our way back to the East Coast with some noses out of joint because only eight of us plus the principals were going to Japan. The plan was that when we arrived in Japan, we would audition Japanese dancers to round out the ensemble, so not everyone was going. After a few days in New York, we boarded a plane bound for Tokyo. My first trip abroad!

# * Chapter 6 *

---

S     even hours by plane to San Francisco, a few hours of
      layover, and another seven hours to Hawaii—this was
      traveling in style! We planned to play a week in Ha-
waii before going on to Japan. We had enlarged our repertory
to include excerpts from *Coppelia*, the Black Swan *pas de deux*,
and a couple of ballets by Slavenska that she had used in her concert company. These had been rehearsed during the end of our
tour in the States. We were put up at the Moana Hotel Cabins.
I didn't regret not staying in the YMCA, although it looked
like a nice one. I hardly remember performing in Honolulu because the week was filled with receptions, sightseeing, enjoying
Waikiki Beach, and eating pineapples. This was a grand prelude
to Japan. Our costumes had been shipped to Hawaii, but we did
not have sets yet because they were to be built in Japan. We used
the curtains and the lights provided by the auditorium.

We left Hawaii late on a Saturday night and woke up a
few hours later on Monday morning, having crossed the
International Date Line on the way to Midway Island, which
was another seven hours ahead of us. Sunday had disappeared.
The menu on the Pan American Clipper was dedicated to us.

"Aloha from the Islands – Slavenska-Franklin Ballet.
Welcome to the Airways of the Orient. Soon your troupe
will enjoy glimpses of Japan where art forms are a matter of

age-old tradition. Even the tea ceremony and moon viewing become Oriental rituals. You'll find Tokyo's audiences cosmopolitan—appreciative of their Noh plays and famous Kabuki theater, but not unaware of the harmonies of our twelve-tone musical scale. Most of all, you'll find the Japanese eager to assimilate Western culture into their post-war national scene. So, we wish you repeated curtain calls and nothing but SRO signs while you are in Japan."

After a brief layover on Midway Island, another five hours brought us to Japan on May 11, 1953. We were the first ballet company to play in Japan. Markova and Dolin had given concerts there but we were the first company. The plane door opened and we were met by representatives of *Mainichi* newspaper, which was sponsoring us. Bouquets were given to the women as we were ushered into convertibles. We were in a motorcade, their version of a Wall Street tickertape parade. It was a far cry from touring by bus.

The stars were put up at the Imperial Hotel while the rest of us stayed at the Hotel Tokyo. The adventures began. Ronnie Colton, my roommate, went into the bathroom to take a shower, and I went downstairs to change some money. At three hundred sixty yen to the dollar, I returned to the room with fistfuls of money that I was tossing in the air when there was a knock on the door. Outside stood eight short Japanese men who bowed to me. I bowed to them, and they marched into the room and sat on the chairs and bed. From my *Japanese in Thirty Hours* book I had learned to say "Watakushi-wa soo-de hako" which meant "I am a box." It didn't seem to be too useful, although if I had known how to say "I'm in a box," it might have been appropriate. After several minutes of their smiling and bowing their heads at me and my smiling and bowing my head at them, one of them pulled blueprints from a canister. Then after grunts, sign language, semaphore, and any other means we could devise, it became clear that they were the stage crew and wanted information about the ballets and the sets which they were building. One of Slavenska's ballets was *Settler's Sunday*, a pastiche of the American West, a minor version of *Rodeo*. Somehow, I managed to convey that it was about cowboys and Indians whereupon the eight Japanese men started running around the room, jumping on the bed, waving imaginary lassoes over their heads, and miming shootouts. That's the scene that greeted Ronnie when he came out of the shower.

The next day we auditioned the Japanese dancers for the company. We hired eight women and one man who were to be used in *Swan Lake* and *The Nutcracker*. I quickly learned to count *ichi, ni, san, shi*, which I equated to "itchy knee without she." It worked—I can still count to four in Japanese.

Ronnie and I moved to the YMCA—habits are hard to break, and it was cheaper. The company rehearsed for a week, and the sets were duplicated with Japanese precision. We were to play at the Imperial Theater which was across the street from the gardens of the Royal Palace. The theater was occupied by the Takarazuka Revue, an all-female group that had two touring troupes plus one at their home base in Takarazuka, an amusement center of theaters, a zoo, and a botanical garden. They had their own enormous theater in Tokyo, but it had been taken over by the U.S. Armed Forces and renamed the Ernie Pyle Theater. Therefore, they were in the Imperial Theater playing only matinees while we did evenings. I went to one of the matinees and saw *The Son of Cho Cho San*, a retelling of *Madame Butterfly*, and when the Cho Cho San character died, she went to heaven on a swing that rose to the flies unevenly, just like Little Eva in the Jack Kelly tent show back in Brown City.

On opening night just before the performance was to begin, Otto Frolich, the conductor, appeared ashen faced. He didn't recognize anyone in the orchestra. They were all new. Evidently it was an honor to be chosen to play in the orchestra, and there were too many musicians to be honored. The solution had been to send some for the rehearsals and others to play the performances. They seemed to think that the rehearsals were for the benefit of the conductor. Somehow, it worked out except one night when they were playing for *Settler's Sunday.* The orchestra split into two, or three, or who knows how many sections. There was a cacophony of sound coming from the pit which was not anything the dancers had heard before. The company was reduced to counting and waiting for the curtain to come down.

Americans applaud during a performance when they like something. Europeans emit a sibilant hiss, which is unnerving until it's explained to you. The Japanese maintain a respectful silence. However, no one explained this custom to us. On opening night, after we ran through the performance to an eerie silence, we all exchanged glances of doom. At the end of the last ballet, we stood in a line and took a bow. As we faced the floor, we tensed because shadows told us things were flying through the air. Tomatoes maybe? Then as we straightened up we saw that the stage was covered with flowers. We were being pelted by carnations.

We were successful. The theater went wild. Danilova was reduced to tears by her reception. Crowds of fans met us at the stage door every night. Even I had fans. Two girls met me at the stage door every night and gave me gloves, dolls, and gardenias, the flower of love. I found it a bit suspicious but reveled in it. When Prince Akihito came to the performance, we were presented to him. There were parties every night. The Japanese were always deferential to us, and no one mentioned the war. It was as if it had never happened, but it was in the back of everyone's mind.

Tea parties in the Royal Gardens. Geisha parties and sight-seeing. An Army officer invited a group of us to his place for sushi, which I had already discovered and did not like. He assured me he would order something special that I would like. When it arrived, I opened the box and looked at what seemed to be three turds. It was rice wrapped in seaweed, and I dutifully ate them hoping I had the correct smile of appreciation on my face. I tried to sit Japanese style at dinners, but always ended up with cramps in my knees. Everything was new and different, and I was having the time of my life. I gorged on large plates of huge strawberries with giant gobs of whipped cream for the grand amount of thirty-three cents. I almost, but not quite, got my fill of strawberries in Japan.

I went to the Kabuki theater, bought a box lunch, and stayed all day. I was mesmerized even though I understood nothing that was happening on stage. I saw the famous scene in which a house was blown away by a hurricane and another in which an actor changes costumes on stage in a blink of an eye.

One night, for a tempura party, Ronnie bought a kimono and a samurai wig, and had himself made up by a makeup artist from the Kabuki. He was already in the restaurant in full regalia when we arrived, and he looked sensational. Danilova took one look at him and said, "Oh, look, it's Ronnie."

News arrived that Flint had been struck by a tornado, and the first word was that it was very serious. My two fans went with me to the Associated Press office to get the latest news, of which there was little. I did not know if I still had a family until an airmail letter from Mom arrived several days later.

At the YMCA, Ronnie and I remarked on how modest the Japanese were. In the communal shower, the men always held a little washcloth in front of them to maintain their modesty. One day, Ronnie returned from the shower laughing and saying, "You know, Gene, they're not modest, they're ashamed." A washcloth had slipped. Later, I was in a pool when two women wearing nothing but washcloths came into the pool. I was not yet enough of a man of the world to get out of the pool while they were there without a washcloth of my own. I had to wait until they were finished to make my escape.

The Korean War was still on but was winding down. After Japan, the company was to go to the Philippines, and negotiations were in process to take us to Korea to entertain the troops. I liked the idea because civilians were not allowed in the war zone, so if we went, we would be made honorary captains for the duration of our stay. I wanted to be a captain, but one of the ballets scheduled was one in which I wore tights, a white periwig, and shoes with heels on them. I looked a little like Dolly Parton on a bad day. The thought of appearing in front of the troops in that outfit was something that I tried unsuccessfully to push from my mind. I could already hear the hoots and catcalls if I appeared in that outfit.

After our week in Tokyo, we boarded a train for Nagoya, Osaka, Takarazuka, and Kyoto. One day in Nagoya, I was in Fred's room when we heard a shriek from Danilova next door. Fred rushed into her room to find her stuck in the bathtub. It was a small tub and in order to use it, one had to sit with one's knees under one's chin. It was easy getting in but difficult to get any leverage to lift yourself out. In Takarazuka, the Americans were given Western style rooms while the Japanese were given traditional rooms with mats, screens, and sliding doors. We immediately switched because we thought the Japanese rooms were great, and the Japanese were happy to try the amenities of the Western rooms. In Kyoto, we were feted in the Royal Gardens and enjoyed more sightseeing of the famous Zen gardens. Then we went back to Tokyo for some performances at the Ernie Pyle Theater, which felt like playing Radio City Music Hall after the smaller theaters we had been playing.

The armistice ending the Korean War was signed, so plans to go to Korea were cancelled. This left with me a free month after the Philippines before a summer tour in the States. I had the idea that since I was already halfway around the world that it would be fun to continue traveling. I rerouted my ticket to go west from Manila. Hong Kong was the midpoint, so I only had to pay the difference between Manila and Hong Kong. It cost me ninety dollars. Most of the company was anxious to get home, but I was having a great time.

We flew to Manila and played a week on a small stage at the Far Eastern University. Manila was depressing. Great stretches of the city had been destroyed in the war. Rubble was lying where it had fallen, and people were living in it. The facades of the hotels were still scarred where they had been hit by artillery shells. In Manila, people were not adverse to talking about the war, and they had nothing good to say about the Japanese. Again, we were partied and ferried around to the sights, but everyone's minds were focused on moving on. Ronnie decided he would go around the world with me and had his ticket rerouted for eighty dollars. (Later, when I got back to New York, I took my ticket to Pan Am and said there was a discrepancy and asked them to check it out. They ended up sending me a check for forty-five dollars, so my trip around the world cost me a grand total of forty-five dollars.)

One night, I was having drinks in a bar with Danilova and Fred. Fred turned to Danilova and said, "Choura, one more drink and you'll be crawling out of this bar." Danilova put a handkerchief on her head, got down on all fours, and said, "Okay, Fredika, I crawl." The Grand Dame was a great sport. There is another story about Danilova, which I don't know is true or not, but I have heard it so many times that I assumed it to be so. Somewhere she had been on stage in her *Swan Lake* costume waiting for the performance to begin. There was a delay in raising the curtain, and Danilova told the stage manager she was going to the bathroom. Shortly after, whatever problems there had been were solved, so the ballet began. The stage manager realized Danilova was absent. He rushed to the bathroom and found her out cold. She had pulled the chain too hard, and the tank had come off the wall, knocking her out.

In Manila, we met a man who worked for the March of Dimes as a reporter. He was a funny Englishman with a large walrus mustache. He told of a time on some assignment when he was approached by a tiny woman who asked, "You're an Englishman, aren't you?"

He proudly pulled himself up to his full height and responded, "Yes, Ma'am, I am." She promptly pulled out a pair of scissors from her purse and cut off his mustache. Snip. Snip. He gave Ronnie and me the names and addresses of a couple of friends to look up in Hong Kong.

The company finished its Manila engagement, and the next day Ronnie and I took off for Hong Kong, landing at that scariest of airports. We checked into the YMCA on Kowloon next to the Peninsula Hotel. The flight schedules were twice a week, so our itinerary was to land in a city and stay two or three days until the next flight going West. We immediately bought tailor made cashmere coats for ourselves and also one for Fred, who had given me the money to buy him one. We explored the city, rode the funicular railroad to Victoria Peak, and looked up the friends whose addresses we had been given. They drove us to Aberdeen for a fish dinner. The next morning while sitting on the john, I thought all of my insides were going to end up in the South China Sea. For the next couple of days, I was never far from a toilet. Ronnie had an opposite reaction. He didn't have a bowel movement until we reached Athens. Fortunately, my affliction started to clear by the time we took off for Bangkok with the advice to look up a certain rickshaw driver named Pon in front of the Tropicana Hotel.

After arriving in exotic Bangkok, we took a taxi into the city, and the first thing we saw was the ubiquitous Coca-Cola sign. Bangkok was the dirtiest city I had ever seen and, at the same time, the most beautiful. Sewage canals ran alongside the roads, but when you turned a corner, in front of you might stand a gorgeous Buddhist temple. The next morning, we came out of our hotel intending to find the Tropicana Hotel to see if we could find Pon. We stopped to ask a rickshaw driver the way to the Tropicana and discovered we had already found Pon. He took us under his wing, and we climbed into his rickshaw to see the sights of Bangkok. We saw the Emerald Buddha and the floating markets, always being pulled through the streets by Pon, an endeavor that embarrassed me. It seemed to us that every step was agony for Pon as he grunted and strained his muscles, but every time he turned around he was smiling. We ended the first day at a square where Pon wanted us to admire the beautiful Thai bobby-soxers. We were way ahead of him because in one look we knew they were drag queens. But, not one was in a Thai costume, all were dressed as American bobby-soxers, a style probably given to them by the U.S. Army during the war. On the second night, Pon wanted to show us something special, so we climbed into his rickshaw and he hauled us a few miles into the countryside. I began to wonder if we were being hijacked. Our destination turned out to be a small house where we were shown a pornographic film about a dog and I don't know how many women. The dog was exhausted by the end of the film. I had come all the way to Bangkok to see a grainy porn film, my first. Maybe Pon had gotten his ideas of American tastes from servicemen. He certainly thought that Ronnie and I had kinky tastes.

We visited a snake farm and saw hundreds of cobras in a pit with a man milking them. This was of particular interest to Ronnie because he had hurt his back in Hawaii and had been given a shot of snake venom as a cure. It hadn't been completely successful because he still had a bad back. As we were ready to leave, Ronnie dropped his tripod on the foot of a man standing next to him. When he picked it up, I noticed that the man had six toes on his foot, and I told Ronnie of my observation. He said, "Really?" and dropped the tripod again so he could get a good look.

We arrived in New Delhi late at night and walked down an unlit street for what seemed like several miles to our third-class hotel. It couldn't have been more romantic, with lots of beaded curtains and overhead fans. Sydney Greenstreet could have been cast as the desk clerk at our hotel. We had a large room with a bath that was a short distance away, out a door and down along a balcony. There was no running water in the rooms or bath. The john was a chair with a pot underneath, which someone else emptied. The bath was a copper tub that a servant filled with warm water if you requested a bath.

I have absolutely no recollection of how we met him, but an Indian man appeared and insisted on showing us New Delhi. Innocent babes have a lot of luck sometimes. On our first day in India, we were chauffeured all over New Delhi. The next day, we boarded a train for Agra. We spent most of the time in the dining car drinking tea. We passed through a sand storm, and every two minutes the waiter wiped off the table. My white trousers turned yellow with sand, and after repeated washings, I threw them away because I could not get the sand out of them.

In Agra, we hired a taxi to take us to the Taj Mahal. Coming down a dusty road, just before we parked, we spied the gleaming white minarets and knew that we had arrived. We walked through a large stone gate, and there it was, the Taj Mahal. The Taj Mahal is one of two things which didn't disappoint me, the other being Michelangelo's *David*, which I later saw in Florence. In Agra, the serenity, the majesty, and the proportions of the Taj Mahal were all truly awe-inspiring. Unfortunately, the inside was covered with graffiti, mostly the "Kilroy was here" variety in many languages.

I once had a friend who when asked, "Guess who I saw today?" always responded, "Margaret Truman." The unexpectedness and familiarity with Miss Truman always received a smile. Well, when Ronnie and I got on the next airplane to fly to Beirut, guess who was sitting in front of us? No, not Margaret Truman, but pretty close—Eleanor Roosevelt and her secretary. This was in the days before planes had different classes. Ronnie asked if he could take pictures with his movie camera, and she graciously allowed it. For the next several hours, I stared at the top of Mrs. Roosevelt's grey head. I tried to eavesdrop, but couldn't hear a thing she and her secretary said.

During our layover in Basra, Mrs. Roosevelt disappeared into a VIP lounge. The rest of us filled out an immigration form and spent our time sitting under the palm trees. Both Ronnie, who was a non-practicing Jew, and I, a non-practicing nothing, had left blank the question on the form regarding our religion. We were called back to the immigration desk and learned that religion was the main point of the paper. So, we both told the officer we were Buddhists, and that seemed to suffice.

Back on the plane, we took off late and were afraid we were going to miss our one day to see Beirut. There was no grey head in front of me, so I thought that Mrs. Roosevelt had stayed in Basra. But, no, the crew had made up a berth for her so that she could sleep from Basra to Beirut. We landed twelve hours late, so in Beirut we had only time to check into a hotel for the night.

The next morning at the Beirut airport, we met Mohammed and Ali. Mohammed had blond hair and blue eyes. Ali was dark and swarthy. They were members of the soccer team from the University of Cairo and were returning to Cairo after a match in Beirut. Wings were spread, and once again, Ronnie and I had our angel guides for our next stop. They were great hosts and insisted on paying for most things, except ice cream. Somehow they had the idea that we loved ice cream and allowed us to pay for any ice cream we bought. We agreed that when they came to America, we would pay for everything except ice cream, which they would buy. It was a nice arrangement and allowed us to go many places we wouldn't ordinarily have gone.

We climbed the pyramids, rode camels (their faces always remind me of Loretta Young for some reason), and went to the spectacular National Museum, although we were beginning to feel saturated by sightseeing. We went to the bazaar and bought perfume "made especially for us and matching our personalities," and it wasn't much of a compliment. Mohammed and Ali told us that when you want water in a Cairo restaurant, you call "Mohammed," and if no one comes, you yell "Ali."

It's always one or the other. They took us to their athletic club on the Nile, and we swam in the river, only to learn later on that wasn't the smartest thing to do. Fortunately, we had no repercussions. They initiated us into the Egyptian custom of male friends holding hands when they walked in the streets. Ronnie took some film of Mohammed and I holding hands as we walked along the Nile. When I began filming Ali and Ronnie, they came to a pole and had to separate, so only I was immortalized in the compromising position. Ronnie told me that when he had shown the film, no one had ever made a comment.

One afternoon in the hotel, we heard a strange sound coming from the street. When we looked out, we saw a parade for a recently deceased general led by Muhammad Naguib, the first President of Egypt. The sound we heard was the slow and measured "clomp" of the soldiers' boots. There was no other sound as the parade passed. I found it very impressive. We left Cairo with promises to Mohammed and Ali that we would see them sometime in the States. We flew on to Athens. Mohammed called my telephone number a couple of years later, but I was in Europe at the time.

In Rome, we ran into company members from Ballet Theatre who were there on tour. We saw two of their performances at an outdoor theater. One was strictly amateur night, and the other was absolutely brilliant. I had never seen a company that could be so radically different from night to night. Dutiful dancers that we were—Ronnie and I had packed shoes, tights, and dance belts—we took a class with the company. Afterwards, we did more sightseeing, which was getting tiresome, but you had to do it when you had the chance. We also took a day trip to Venice, and then we left for Paris.

In Paris, we checked into the Hotel Mont Joli on Rue Fromentin near Place de Clichy, the first stop for most expatriate dancers in Paris. There we found Jaime Bauer who had not been included in the Japanese tour and had moved to Paris in the meantime. We had a whole week to spend in Paris to rejuvenate and enjoy. I started dreamily making plans to live in Paris someday.

Every morning, we went to Studio Wacker to take class with Madame Nora. Her studio was much smaller than I was used to. There was no space to practice leaps. My pirouettes weren't so hot, but Madame Nora liked my approach and asked where I had learned it. When I told her I had learned it from Slavenska, she nodded approvingly. The Studio Wacker was the center of the dance world in Paris and had an infamous WC. It was literally a closet containing a porcelain bowl with two raised foot prints in the floor and a chain to flush the overhead tank. The problem arose when one finished and pulled the chain. It was first necessary to step out of the closet because if you remained on the foot prints when you pulled the chain, the water would rise around your ankles. Newcomers frequently announced themselves with a shriek from the WC. The first shriek I heard was my own.

I covered all the tourist attractions including the Follies Bergère with Yvonne Printemps. I learned to eat European style by not changing the fork to the right hand and thought it was the height of sophistication. However, I've never managed to eat peas in this manner. I still put my fork in the right hand and use it as a spoon. My Uncle Hub used to eat peas with a knife. Now that's sophistication.

Our last stop was London just days after the coronation of Queen Elizabeth II. The decorations were still up, and London was very festive. Ronnie and I had tacitly agreed to go our own way in London. We hadn't had any arguments; we were just tired of each other and ready for some alone time, so I explored London by myself.

Afterwards, it was time to get home for rehearsals of the summer engagements. I arrived at Idlewild, which was later re-named John F. Kennedy International, on a Saturday evening. I had flown around the world—not bad for a twenty-two-

year-old kid from Brown City who used to think going on a
Greyhound bus was an adventure.

The next day I rushed to the beach at Riis Park, planning
to answer my friends', "Where have you been?" with, "Around
the world!" Unfortunately, it was not a good beach day, and
none of my friends were there to ask where I had been. My flip
reply remained in my pocket.

# * Chapter 7 *

The Eisenhower-Stevenson campaign was in full swing when I got back to New York, but I had more important things to focus on—a summer tour of outdoor theaters with the company. There wasn't much of a company left, so it had to be rebuilt and rehearsed. Ballet companies tend to be fluid. Most of the members who had not gone to Japan were working elsewhere or not interested. Some of the company who had gone to Japan were tired of the whole thing and were off to other things. Fortunately, Sally Streets had joined the New York City Ballet and was a marvelously bright light.

Somewhere along the line, a friend of mine had met a woman named Ryllis Hasoutra and started to drag me along when he went to visit her. She had been an exotic dancer in the twenties, had traveled the world, and was a brilliant *raconteur*. Evenings spent in her apartment were filled with wonderful stories of the famous, and her stories were first hand. If Hasoutra was telling a story about Charlie Chaplin, it had happened at her dinner table. If she was talking about Richard Haliburton, it was because he had been her next-door neighbor. One night, a pleasantly plump, overly rouged, elderly woman was present. She turned out to be Rosetta Duncan, one of the Duncan Sisters, a famous vaudeville act. I thought that she had already died. You never knew who might turn up as Hasoutra's. And, it being the Fifties and the age of McCarthyism, it was enough to make your armpits tingle to know that Alger Hiss lived in the apartment above Hasoutra's.

Auditions were held, new dancers were hired, and rehearsals began. A couple of new ballets were added to the repertoire, and then we were on the bus again with the same tyrant driving us. Boris Runanin, another Yugoslavian and former Ballet Russe member, had joined us as a principal and a choreographer. We also picked up another new principal dancer, a wealthy woman from Texas who had infused the company with some cash for the promise of a few performances.

Performing outdoors was strange. There were so many distractions—airplanes zooming overhead, bugs zooming around your head, wind in the trees. More than one fly had been consumed unexpectedly while gasping for breath. At the Red Rocks Amphitheater outside of Denver, there was wind. It was so strong that a leap forward was likely to land you exactly where you had started. When the stagehands put four doors on castors in place for *Streetcar*, there was a gasp from the audience. The stagehands were walking off stage, and the doors were following right behind them. Dancers who were not in *Streetcar* were dressed in black tights and leotards, and we held the doors in place and helped move them when cast members changed the position of the doors on stage. That night, the audience saw strange figures in black, bent over, and scooting around the stage trying to look small and invisible. It probably gave new symbolism to the ballet.

Summer passed. We rehearsed a couple of new ballets to fill out the repertoire and were on the road again for a fall tour. As we neared the end of the tour, we began sinking, slowly but inexorably. Audiences were sparse and after we played our last date in Columbus, Ohio, we were dead. I ended my time with Slavenska by riding in the back of a truck, trying to keep the tarp over the scenery as we took it back to New York down the Pennsylvania Turnpike, and wondering if the Turnpike Sniper was out that night. There had been a rash of sniper shootings on the Turnpike that year.

It had been a wonderful year and a half. I'd gained experience, traveled the world, worked with professionals, made new friends all over the world. I'd been partied, saw my first jug band playing music with jugs, spoons, and saws at a reception outside Louisville, Kentucky, met royalty and the famous, and now it was over. Now what? My only real hope of employment was the rumor that Ballet Russe was re-forming, and maybe I'd have a chance at that. Later, talking with Fred who had rejoined the Ballet Russe, I got the impression that I had been expected to go along, but no one ever told me.

Things turned out to be not so bleak. John Butler hired me for a season at the New York City Opera. Actually, he hired me to do a concert and the Opera gave us a paycheck. I knew nothing about opera and could not keep one separate from the other. *Carmen*, I knew. That was the one in which Felisa Conde and I rolled around on the floor as the curtain went up. John's wonderful dances for *La Cenerentola* were distinctive, and I knew the dances for the premier of Copeland's *The Tender Land* and *Amahl and the Night Visitors*. As for the minuets and court dances for *Don Giovani*, I knew not one from the other and always had to ask what we did next. But I do remember Beverly Sills in the chorus. Not so much her voice, which I probably never heard distinctly, but there was something about her "persona" that I always noticed.

I did my first television performance when John Butler used us on an *Omnibus* show. I splurged and called home to alert Mom to watch. I didn't know that we were going to perform a pantomime behind a scrim and that our shadows would be projected onto the scrim. That's what Mom and her friends in Flint saw. She probably claimed that she could recognize my shadow.

The world of ballet continued to expand. After the Metropolitan Opera opened their new ballet school, Ballet Theatre opened theirs, and then the Ballet Russe opened a school. For political reasons as well as curiosity, I took classes at all of them. I'd fall in love with one person's class and take it for a while until I became entranced with someone else. They all had their idiosyncrasies. Anatole Vilzak always gave combinations from the left, never from the right. Madame Schollar taught while wearing bloomers under her skirt. I had no idea where she got bloomers; maybe she made her own. Madame Anderson taught in the dining room of her apartment on West Fifty-Sixth Street and did not allow us to use resin on our shoes. Instead she had her famous watering can with which she'd dampen the floor to make it less slippery. George Chaffee taught his classes in the apartment below Madame Anderson's. He gave a barre class that was so tricky and complicated that your brain got more of a workout than your body. In his huge studio next to Carnegie Hall, Chester Hale taught by using a metronome for the barre and records for the floor work. That "tick, tick, tick" during the barre was like Chinese water torture. But he did teach me "beats" by having me hang onto rings that hung on heavy elastic from the ceiling. These gave me enough extra support in the air to get the timing right. Most teachers were jealous and did not like their students taking other teacher's classes. If they shared a studio with other teachers, they were very much aware of who was taking whose class. I took Caton's class at Ballet Theatre, and one day when I took Valentina Pereyaslavec's class she asked me, "Why you take my class, the Caton die?" I got the impression that I was welcome, but only if I gave up Caton's class.

I went to Nenette Charrise, whose class was populated with Broadway gypsies. Nenette was a gorgeous, voluptuous woman who was part of the famed Charisse family. Cyd Charisse had been married to Nenette's brother and had kept the name. Nenette's sister, Rita, was a dancer, but Nenette wasn't. She taught. Nenette had a kinesthetic sense that was phenomenal. She could look at you and say, "Pull here," as she touched a rib or a back muscle and everything would fall into place. Her class was very social and relaxed. If you wanted a cigarette after the barre, you could have a cigarette. If you wanted to be left alone, you were left alone. If you wanted to work, she worked you. She was married to Robert Tucker, who frequently worked as Jerome Robbins's assistant, and was *au courante* about what was or was not happening around Broadway. Nenette was popular with modern dancers like Pearl Lang and Sophie Maslov, and even with non-dancers like Mary Martin, Nancy Walker, and Dick Button. Doris Duke turned up in her class. Miss Duke would arrive in front of the studio in her Rolls, get out, walk into the studio, shed her furs, and be ready for class.

Ballet is a unique profession in that it connects you so directly to the past. You are taught by legends in their own right or people who have worked with legends. Style and technique is passed directly from one generation to the next, and until the advent of video tape, the only way to learn an old ballet was from the memory of someone who had performed it. The anecdotal stories and style of the teachers directly connect the students to the past.

Peter Gennaro was teaching jazz so I started taking his classes. They, too, were filled with gypsies and celebrities. For a time, Peter's class was right after Nenette's and in the same studio. Sometimes you'd see Doris Duke walking out of Nenette's class as Grace Kelly and Rita Gam were walking into Peter's.

I went to all the auditions that were announced and never got called back for the finals, although I did stay longer and longer before being eliminated. Ballet Theatre had audition classes that I took and never got a nibble. Neither Lucia Chase nor Agnes de Mille ever seemed to notice me even if I was standing right in front of them. Ronnie had gotten an audition with Balanchine and was now a part of the New York City Ballet. One day, I heard that there was an audition for the New York City Ballet, so I went over to the School of American

Ballet, the affiliated school where I had never taken a class. Balanchine gave us a class as an audition. I left thinking, "Well, at least I had a free class." That night Vida Brown, the Ballet Mistress, called and said Mr. Balanchine had decided to go with me. I couldn't have been more surprised or terrified.

The New York City Ballet had been formed in 1948. The performance I saw during my first week in New York in 1949 was part of its second season. Since then, it had grown and become a celebrated company. All listings I saw from Europe ranked it as the best company in the world, although the lists from the States ranked it behind the Bolshoi and Royal Ballet. The company had a wonderful roster of ballerinas: Maria Tallchief, Tanaquil LeClerq, Melissa Hayden, Janet Reed, Patricia Wilde, each of them spectacular and distinctive. The men, if not great technicians, were good partners capable of marvelous dramatic performances. They included Nicholas Magallanes, Francisco Moncion, Herbert Bliss, Todd Bolender, and the new sensation, Jacques D'Amboise. Then Andre Eglevsky joined the company, and they had a first-rate premier *danseur* with an exceptional technique. One year, it seemed as if Ballet Theatre was being denuded as Nora Haye, Anthony Tudor, Hugh Laing, and Diana Adams left Ballet Theatre to join the New York City Ballet. Even Harold Lang, a Broadway dancing star, joined the company for a brief time.

George Balanchine was the star and principal choreographer, but he had help from Jerome Robbins creating new ballets for the company such as *The Cage*, *Fanfare*, and *Afternoon of a Faun*. When Tudor joined the company, he brought with him some of his ballets. Frederic Ashton, the great English choreographer, created such ballets as *Illuminations* and *Picnic at Tintagel* for the company. It seemed as if all the great creative forces of Western ballet were centered with the New York City Ballet.

The Ballet performed at the City Center on Fifty-Fifth Street. It was an old Masonic Temple that had been bought by the city, which then rented it to the City Center for a nominal fee of one dollar per year. The City Center was established as a people's theater with several constituents providing year-round entertainment at a three-dollars-fifty-cents top ticket. There were sessions of the New York City Opera Company and a series of revivals of plays with major stars such as Tallulah Bankhead in *A Streetcar Named Desire,* or Orson Welles in *King Lear,* which he did in a wheelchair, having broken his leg. There were revivals of musicals with major stars. It was a beehive of theatrical activity.

The New York City Ballet had two seasons, Spring and Fall. As their audience grew, the seasons became longer, but there were limits because the theater was booked for operas and plays. It's hard to keep a company together for a season of four to six weeks plus rehearsals and several weeks of unemployment before the next rehearsal period. Therefore, the company toured a lot. When the theater was not available, it went to Chicago, the West Coast, or Europe. By doing so, the company was kept together and built a reputation.

It was an exciting time. The opening of each season and the premier of a new work, of which there were two, three, or four per season, was like a Broadway opening. The chic people were there. The balletomanes were there. It was the place to be on any particular night. I remember sitting on the floor in Martha Graham's class when she stopped the class and told us that we must see Maria Tallchief in *The Firebird.* In her opinion, it was one of the great theatrical performances of all time. In the Spring season of 1954, Balanchine introduced his full-length *Nutcracker* with thirty performances to critical and public favor. A tradition was born.

This was what I was joining, and I felt ill-prepared with only four years of study and having started dancing late in life. For years, one of the guys, who was at the audition where I was chosen and who didn't get the job, told me that Balanchine had made a mistake at that audition, and that he should have gotten the job. I never knew if he remembered that I was the one who beat him out or not, and I'm not at all sure that he wasn't right. I was very insecure of my expertise, so I started taking classes at the School of American Ballet. This had had two great perks— classes were free to the company, and you always had a supply of dance shoes.

The School of American Ballet was at Fifty-Ninth Street and Madison Avenue, set apart from the usual dance district around Carnegie Hall. The school's executive director was Eugenie Ouroussow, a princess of the Romanov family. The teachers at the school were all wonderful characters. There was Anatole Oboukoff, married to ballerina Vera Nemtchinova, Pierre Vladimiroff, married to Felica Doubrovska, and Muriel Stuart, a grand, chic lady who had danced with Pavlova.

Oboukoff's class began before you saw him. As soon as he entered a small vestibule that led to the studio, he said in his gruff voice, "one" and the *pliés* began. He was a taskmaster and always exuded an attitude that teaching us to dance was a formidable and futile job. I think that I never saw him smile. If there was a new student in class, he would stand next to him or her at the barre and snap his fingers about an eighth of an inch in front of their nose. I think that maybe I got on his good side by cracking a slight but not disrespectful smile when he did this to me. In one of my first classes with him, a class in which I was particularly inept, he stopped the class and asked Jacques D'Amboise if I was new to the company. Jacques verified that I was. Oboukoff called me over to stand in front of him. While sitting on a bench in front of the class, he asked in his heavily accented Russian voice, "You dance with New York City Ballet?"

I would have denied it except that Jacques had just confirmed the fact and responded, "Yes." He looked at me slowly shaking his head then looked at the floor as if ballet was doomed. I was looking for a hole into which I could disappear. His criticism of me was so harsh that one day his wife, Nemtchinova, who was in class, said to me, "You like my husband? I tell him *you're good boy.*"

It wasn't necessary. I adored the man and knew that even though his criticism was like being hit with a sledgehammer, if he didn't like you, he added a rake after the hammer. His were the toughest classes I have ever taken. The only way I got through them was that he gave a long "adagio" that gave the second group a few moments to rest while the first group worked. It was rumored that he had once broken a girl's jaw while yanking it into the correct position.

Vladimiroff was the opposite. He was a kind, gentle man who entered the studio with an apologetic "good morning" in a tiny voice. Sometimes it took several tiny "good mornings" to realize he was there. He had replaced Nijinsky in many of Nijinsky's roles and specialized in male techniques. He was forever explaining that the heels of Nijinsky's shoes were never dirty because only his forefeet touched the ground.

Doubrovska was a tall, thin, bird-like woman who had the original role of the siren in *Prodigal Son*. I avoided her classes, thinking they were geared towards women. I liked Muriel Stuart. A tall, elegant woman with a ramrod straight spine, she had the air of a *grande dame*. She always wore an ankle length black skirt and a sweater buttoned over one shoulder so that the sleeves trailed down her back. One day during barre exercise, she was walking along the barre, counting to the music, "One, two, three, four...." Suddenly, she broke wind and the class started to giggle. Without missing a beat and in meter she said, "I'm only human...seven, eight." The mantra of dancers. I hate to think of the number of times I've counted to four or eight in my lifetime. Another day, I was watching her class from the bench in front of the studio. She was correcting one of the girls. "That's right, dear, ah, just so... beautiful dear." She then swooped and sat down beside me, being careful of her elegant line and said in a low voice, "Poor dear, can't stand on two legs."

The company's professional class at the school was always exciting. It was filled with the famous of the past, present, and future. Balanchine had been married five times, all to ballerinas—

Danilova, Tamara Geva, Vera Zorina, Maria Tallchief, and his current wife, Tanaquil LeClerq. At various times, I saw combinations of four in class, although I never saw all five in the same class.

After the company class, which was not required but made good sense and good politics to attend, came rehearsals, the schedule for which was posted on a bulletin board in the lobby. I was inserted into the repertoire in such ballets as *Swan Lake*, *Bourree Fantasque*, *Symphony in C*, *Fanfare*, and *The Pied Piper* for the winter season. The season closed with two weeks of *Nutcracker*, which drove the company crazy. Being a repertory company, we were not used to doing the same thing night after night. I was happy as a lark—I had a job with an esteemed company, even though I sometimes felt like an interloper. I worked hard and had thoughts of doing some particular roles. Vida Brown, the ballet mistress, conducted the rehearsals. Balanchine would come in to polish and sometimes change steps. I wasn't included in any of the new ballets, so I didn't see much of "Mr. B."

New York City Ballet at that time consisted of about forty to forty-five dancers—twenty girls, nine boys, twelve principals, and five featured performers. To me, women in ballet make-up are always beautiful. For rehearsals, the women were divided into two groups, short and tall. About half of the men were homosexual. Of the other half, half were married to women in the company, and most of the rest had long-term relationships outside the company. It was not a promiscuous lot. Homosexuality was tacitly accepted but seldom referred to openly. I had heard, but do not really know, that Balanchine disapproved. However, the management always seemed to know who were having relationships, and couples were put in the same roomettes on the trains. Trains had upgraded to roomettes from Pullmans. Frequently, the first I knew that certain relationships had changed, was when I got on the train and different people were sharing different roomettes. It was a sure sign. Whether the wonderful Betty Cage and Barbara Horgan had been informed of the shifting alliances or had more sensitive ears to the ground than did I, remained a mystery.

After the season, there was a layoff. That was the story of the ballet—rehearsals, seasons, then unemployment insurance of thirty dollars a week. On one layoff, I finished the week and still had five dollars left. It became my code of honor to save five dollars out of the unemployment check. Somewhere along the way, Rod Alexander called me to do a Max Liebman special on television. It was a musical version of *The Grand Tour*, and I, with seven other guys, did a number in a French bistro with Tammy Grimes before she became famous for *The Unsinkable Molly Brown*. This time Mom could see me.

Two of the company members were Barbara Fallis and Dick Thomas who had met and married while dancing for Alicia Alonso in Cuba. Their son, Richard, who had a mole on his cheek, became very famous as John-Boy on *The Waltons*. The Thomas household was a mélange of Diana the Great Dane, a poodle, a bird, and an assortment of Cuban refugee dancers. One night, Dick was reading and noticed that the bird was sitting on Diana's shoulder. He went back to reading. Gradually he became aware of burping sounds and looked up to see Diana burping feathers. After years of sharing the same apartment, Diana had eaten the bird. On tour, Barbara, Dick, Richard, and Diana all managed to squeeze into one compartment.

I joined the company in the spring of 1954 in time for a tour to Chicago and the West Coast which ended with our playing *The Nutcracker* at the Greek Theatre in Los Angeles, where we were given free rein of the pool at a private residence. One day, when a group of us arrived at the pool, we found Judith Anderson sitting on the porch of the guesthouse. Miss Statue of Liberty was taking a break. During this tour, we rehearsed a new Balanchine ballet called *Western Symphony*. Up until this time, I had only seen Balanchine rehearse and polish old ballets. This was the first time that I was in on the creation.

It's hard to realize that his genius was so simple. No breast beating, no tantrums, no angst. He would come into the studio, talk a bit of small talk, maybe about a meal he had had last night, ask the pianist to play a few bars of music, place some dancers in positions, name some steps while demonstrating with his hands, then ask the dancers to do it. After, the process would repeat, and before you knew it, he had completed a section of the ballet. It seemed so simple that anyone could do it. I never saw him yell at anyone. He always gave encouragement. Being ignored was the only sign of disfavor. Of course, he was held in such awe by the dancers that no one deliberately crossed him.

Back in New York for the season at the City Center, I heard "it" for the second time. But this time I was on stage, not in the wings. At the end of our first movement of *Western Symphony*, we hit our final poses, and it was a wonder that the dome didn't blow off the City Center. That joyous slap in the face! From then on through the rest of the ballet, we knew we had a new hit.

We also rehearsed and premiered *Ivesiana* to the music of Charles Ives. The piece I was in was *The Unanswered Question* that had four boys carry Allegra Kent, the emerging ballerina, around the stage. We carried her on our shoulders, wound her around our bodies and through our legs, never letting her touch the floor while Todd Bolender crawled around the stage in front of us. We had no idea what it was all about, and nobody could count the music. Only near the end when we heard a trumpet in the orchestra did we know that we were either late or ahead of ourselves. I got my picture in Time Magazine when they did a big story on us.

Then we did an unprecedented seven-week season of *The Nutcracker* during the Christmas season. The company, used to repertory, went bonkers doing the same thing every night. I drew lines on my face and tried to walk "old" in the first act as the Grandfather, and then did *Chocolate* in the second act. With Slavenska, I had done *Tea*, the Chinese dance. The kid from Brown City was in the middle of things.

# * Chapter 8 *

*A*fter a short respite, we began rehearsals for the spring season. This time Balanchine was doing *Roma* to Bizet's music, with sets by Eugene Berman, plus a *pas de trois* from the *Glinka*. Robbins did *The Concert*, a genuinely comic ballet. On the first day of rehearsals, Balanchine lined us up and brought another guy and myself forward, not as featured roles, just to do a few steps by ourselves. Did Balanchine like me? Was he grooming me? Ah, hopes! My career was moving forward. One day in Peter Gennaro's jazz class, Peter suggested that I audition for his role in the road company of *Pajama Game* doing the famous "Steam Heat" number with Carol Haney, Buzz Miller, and Peter. I was torn, but considering that Balanchine seemed to have some interest in me, I decided that I'd better stay where I was.

I was excited to work for Jerome Robbins in *The Concert*. He was my ballet hero. His *The Guests* had been on the program the first time I saw the New York City Ballet. I loved *Afternoon of a Faun*, *The Cage*, *The Pied Piper*, and *Fanfare* and was thrilled when the company revived *The Age of Anxiety*, although when Janet Reed, who had left the company, came in and saw what we were rehearsing, she said, "Don't they know that age is over?" Janet or otherwise, I liked the ballet. I felt an affinity for his work and loved dancing it. He was also the preeminent choreographer on Broadway, which had kept him busy since I had been with the company. *The Concert* was my first opportunity to work for him.

Rehearsing with Jerry was a lot different than rehearsing for Balanchine. Jerry created several versions of *The Concert*, and then we rehearsed putting the first part of Version C with the second part of Version A, then the first part of Version A with the middle of Version C, ending with Version B. It kept us on our toes, excuse the pun. It turned out to be very successful, and it remains one of the few truly comic ballets.

One day while rehearsing *Roma*, the door to the studio opened. In walked Igor Stravinsky, Eugene Berman and his wife, Ona Munson, who portrayed Belle Watling in *Gone with the Wind*. When you associate with the great, you never know whom you're going to meet. Sadly, Miss Munson committed suicide a few weeks later. Berman had designed the set of an Italian piazza with laundry hanging between the houses. Later, when we played the ballet in Italy, the laundry was missing. It was thought that it might be insulting to Italians. We were politically correct three decades before it was politically correct to be politically correct.

When the season ended, we headed for a three-month tour of Europe, opening in Monte Carlo at its gem of an opera house, just above the railroad station where Fred Franklin had stood as World War II started. Monte Carlo, where Moira Shearer had thrown herself over the balcony at the end of *The Red Shoes*. Monte Carlo with its famous casino. I think Somerset Maugham called Monte Carlo a "sunny place for shady people." We weren't shady, but we were a little broke because we were on reduced salary in Europe—the union had deemed living expenses to be less in Europe. We made eighty-five dollars a week. No matter, there were things to see and savor. My new trunk would gather lots of hotel stickers and look very worldly.

Andre Eglevky usually danced a *pas de deux* on our programs, either the *Glinka* or *Minkus*. Andre did not like dancing the

*Glinka*, and whenever it was scheduled, he arrived at the theater complaining that a bad knee made it impossible for him to dance the *Glinka* and that the *Minkus* would have to be substituted. That meant that the concertmaster had to change all the music, which was a general annoyance to the musicians. One night when the *Glinka* was scheduled, the conductor, Leon Berzin, arrived at the theater with his arm in a sling and said he couldn't conduct the *Minkus*, it would have to be the *Glinka*. I don't remember the resolution—maybe that night they did *Sylvia*.

Until Baryshnikov, Eglevsky had the most perfect male technique I had seen. Always hitting fifth position, he had wonderful feet and eccentric hands. He possessed multiple pirouettes and *balonne*, that process of seemingly sitting in the air. It's a matter of timing, and no one seems to work on it these days. Andre had passed it on to Jacques D'Amboise and Jacques to his son, Christopher, who unfortunately stopped dancing early.

Melissa Hayden was near perfection in technique and had a dramatic talent as well as a theatrical persona. I suspect that Balanchine didn't really like her style, but she was so good and so popular that he could not deny her stardom.

Patricia Wilde's technique and physicality were spectacular, but she did not have the Balanchine physique because she tended to appear slightly overweight.

Then there was Tanaquil LeClerq. Tanny had an eccentric quality that was unique. Her adagios were sustained and beautiful. During her allegro, there was a glint of mischievousness that was delectable. The lady put on fabulous makeup that was individualized for each role. She was a wonderful talent.

Diana Adams was divinely lyrical with a magnificent long line but she tended to be too careful. Nicholas Magallanes was everyone's favorite partner and was very effective in dramatic roles as was Francisco Moncion.

Today the company is twice as large as during my tenure. I think there is no doubt that, principals excepted, they are technically superior to the dancers of my day, but they seem to have lost some theatricality. Of course, my teachers said the same thing about my generation—that we had no sense of style and personality. Probably, thirty years from now, the same comments will be made. It's no wonder that today's dancer is better—they start younger and are molded earlier. When I danced, there wasn't an adequate school in every mid-sized city and most people weren't aware of ballet. We were the American pioneers. Years later, I met Francisco Moncion on his way to rehearsal at Lincoln Center, and he said that the company was like a factory. He didn't know the people and was never introduced to new members of the company, which by then had numbered around a hundred. Something has to be lost when you don't know the people with whom you're performing. Sociability and camaraderie influence one performer's attitude towards another.

There is a constant war between choreographers and performers. Most good choreographers want their choreography to speak for itself. It's their baby and they want it to succeed or fail on its own. Performers want to express themselves through the choreography and win their own laurels.

During a performance of *Cakewalk*, a button on my jacket caught in the embroidery of my partner's costume. As we twisted and turned, the embroidery started to pull off her costume and tie us in knots. Try as I might, I could not break the embroidery, so by the end of the ballet, we were wrapped in yards of colored thread. As the tour went on, I became aware that either this same girl was overeating, or I was getting weaker because lifting her to my shoulder took all my strength. Her waist started to feel strangely solid, and I started to suspect that I was partnering two for the price of one. It turned out to be true, and she left the company at the end of the tour.

In Marseilles, I tried bouillabaisse for the first time. Not being a fish lover, I was not too impressed. An Englishman who was teaching in Marseilles asked me to speak to his Anglo-Franco group so they could practice their English. There I met the Comte de Catalan and his American poetess wife. They had met through correspondence and had been married by proxy before they ever met in person. He was gregarious and quite fond of Pernod, which he introduced me to. She was a teetotaler, a mouse of a woman who seldom said a word, while we knocked them down beside the old port as he waited for a visa to the States. I think there may be a lot of counts sitting in the bars of Europe. I drank Pernod for years because I liked the taste, and I thought it gave me a *je ne sais quoi* quality.

Jerome Robbins' photograph was in the brochure, although he was not on the tour. Coming out of the stage door, fans constantly presented me with his picture to autograph thinking I was Robbins, although we didn't look very much alike. It was a bother trying to explain in German, French, or Italian, none of which I spoke, that I was not Robbins. So, I started signing his autograph. Sorry, Jerry, there are a lot of fake autographs of yours out there.

Three months filled with Marseilles, Lyon, Florence, Rome, Bordeaux, Lisbon, Paris, Lausanne, Zurich, Stuttgart, Amsterdam, and The Hague. I saw grand opera houses, went to embassy receptions, visited museums, and ate new and different foods. Some of us took a boat up the Rhine from Stuttgart to Amsterdam to see the castles. If receptions were in the morning, we ate like birds. If receptions were after a performance, we attacked the buffets like locusts. In Bordeaux, the stage boards were loose, and when somebody stepped on one end of a board it was likely to pop out and sit on the stage. By the end of a ballet, the stage was strewn with loose boards. The pool in Stuttgart, instead of being populated with blond, blue-eyed Aryans, was filled with short, potato sack bodies, many with missing limbs. Merle Oberon, looking absolutely gorgeous, turned up at a reception at the United States Embassy in Paris. At the airport in Lisbon, I was picked up by a guy in an Alpha-Romeo and thought I was about to be entertained royally until he started to pump me for information about Jillana, a beautiful featured dancer. He had seen her picture and was determined to romance her. He even made a trip to New York to push his case, unsuccessfully.

In Lisbon, we performed once a day, either a matinee at six o'clock or an evening performance at ten o'clock. Every day after class, I boarded the train for Estoril and the beach. I lived on ice cream.

On tour, Balanchine taught the company classes. A Balanchine class is not your usual class. He might well spend most of the class on one exercise. Forty minutes doing *tendues*, slowly and precisely, explaining how he wanted them done, why, and how they led to something else. Sometimes his classes were drudgery, and sometimes they were exhilarating.

When the tour was over, we were briefly back in New York and, afterwards, went to the West Coast where we were joined by a new dancer, Arthur Mitchell, the first black dancer in the company. It quickly became apparent that he was being groomed for some of Jacques's roles. Jacques had been promoted to principal, and it was going to be difficult to replace some of his non-principal roles.

In San Francisco, the road company of *Pajama Game* was playing at the Curran, and Lena Horne was appearing at the Fairmont Hotel. A group of us went to see Miss Horne. I was flabbergasted. Lena Horne is the greatest nightclub performer I have ever seen. She is not a "hit you in the face" performer. She sucks her audience into her vortex with the concentration of a Martha Graham. I had never before and have never since seen anything like it. One of our group knew Miss Horne, so I tagged along to her room to meet her. The idol didn't crack. Wrapped in a blue chenille robe and sweating like a truck driver, she graciously received us in her suite and talked small talk. I never heard anything about Lena Horne that would make me think that she was anything other than a great and very talented lady.

During our engagement in San Francisco, I saw T.C. Jones, the female impersonator. I didn't much like drag queens, but

T.C. was something special because he was a truly fine actor. With a wig on his bald head and very little makeup and using his own voice, he would have an audience near tears while doing the "telephone scene" from *The Great Ziegfeld*. Then he turned his wig around to do a hysterical and cleverly dirty take-off of Judy Holiday. Preceding him in this engagement was a young singer with a haunting voice and overly arranged music. T.C. cut his act short to give the young singer more time because Columbia Records executives were there to audition him. A couple of months later, *Chances Are* was filling the airwaves. The young singer was Johnny Mathis.

San Francisco was always fun to play. There was always so much going on in the city. The North Beach clubs offered a variety of entertainment that went on until the wee hours. Among others, Maya Angelou was playing The Purple Onion and Bob Newhart was at the Hungry I.

In Los Angeles, I went to see Gilda Grey and her shimmy at the Turnabout Theatre. The Turnabout was so named because the auditorium had two stages, one at either end of the auditorium. The first act was played on one stage, and during the intermission the seats were turned around, and the second act was played on the other stage. Gilda Grey was making a comeback. I knew her name, but she hadn't performed in many years, so I was curious to see her. The other half of the program was the wonderful dance satirist, Lotte Goslar, who I had not seen either. While waiting for the performance to begin, I became aware that a lot of the audience was directing its attention to the man sitting next to me. He was not familiar to me, but during intermission, I learned that I was sitting next to someone named Liberace.

Then we were back in New York for a fall season with premiers of Todd Bolender's *Souvenirs* and a cooperative endeavor by several choreographers of *Jeux d'Enfants*, which was never seen again. Maria Tallchief left the company to go with Ballet Russe. The rumor was that she had asked for so much money from Ballet Russe that she had never expected them to accept. When they accepted, she was happily stuck with the arrangement.

My large nose had a big bump on it that I did not like. Ronnie had removed an even bigger bump on his nose. I decided to have a nose job. I used Ronnie's doctor in Detroit. I watched the whole process through one eye except when they started to hit me with a small mallet to break the nose. At that point, I had both eyes closed. After my swollen black eyes and my swollen nose improved, I was pleased with my new look. I was able to spend a week at home, the longest time I'd been there in a long time. One morning, we heard that the *Andrea Doria* had been struck by the *Stockholm* and was sinking. That night, we watched the event on television. The world was changing, and news coverage was becoming immediate. Now, if only I could solve the problem of my hair falling out. I went for scalp treatments that consisted of burning the scalp with a terrible smelling concoction once a week. It didn't help, but I had nice company because sometimes Karl Malden was in the next chair.

I had been subletting an apartment from another dancer who was on tour. He, unfortunately, was returning, and I had to vacate. I noticed and responded to an ad in the paper for a rent controlled apartment. The man I met was the leaseholder, not the landlord. His deal was for me to buy his furniture in exchange for the landlord's address. He was asking four hundred dollars for a desk and chair, two handmade bookcases, a love seat, and a couple of filthy carpets. I offered him a hundred and fifty. He accepted, either because it was the only offer he had, or he wanted out fast. I went to see the landlord who asked me how much I had paid for the furniture. He had seen the ad and knew the whole story. I told him the truth, and he gave me a lease.

I now had the most valuable New York commodity, a rent controlled apartment. I paid fifty-four dollars a month for three rooms on the third floor on Eighty-Third Street between

Columbus and Amsterdam Avenues. It came equipped with its share of cockroaches too. It was also conveniently only one block away from the new studios of the School of American Ballet at Eighty-Third and Broadway. I was no longer a vagabond—I had a permanent address. I found a roommate with whom to share the exorbitant rent. His name was Fergus Hunter. He worked at Variety Arts, a rehearsal studio where many Broadway and television shows rehearsed. We were good friends for many years.

The company was on a hiatus until mid-summer, and I was lucky to pick up a revival of *Kiss Me Kate* with Kitty Carlisle at the City Center, part of their series of musical revivals. After *Kiss Me Kate*, ballet rehearsals started for another European tour. My new nose made its debut. Mr. Balanchine noticed it but didn't comment. I had the impression that he was not very pleased. Mr. Obukoff took one long look. Never one to mince words, he said, "Awful." This tour was to play many of the European festivals—the Biennale in Venice, the Oktoberfest in Munich, and another one in Salzburg, where we opened in late August. This time the union had won us the same pay as we got in the States.

Several annoying things happened on this tour. The first thing happened to my trunk. When it was being unloaded, it was dropped. It was easily repaired, but the side with all my hotel stickers was ruined so I had to start all over again. Then a role I had understudied was given to someone else, so my new nose was a little out of joint. There were also nice things such as the small, dirty john in the Venice Theater that had a great view of the rooftops of Venice. Taking a gondola in a canal to the hotel when we arrived in Venice was amazing. I saw Jacques D'Amboise dance in the Piazza San Marco.

While playing Salzburg, I spent a glorious day at the Eagle's Nest, Hitler's retreat. When I arrived, there were only a few people there, so I had the place to myself. It was a clear day. I sat for hours looking out over the valley until clouds moved in below me. I had the almost uncontrollable urge, which I fortunately controlled, to jump into those clouds. They looked like a soft bed you could bounce on. I've never worried about the psychology of it, but I'm glad I didn't jump.

We took a boat trip down the Danube from Salzburg to Vienna. We started off very comfortable with lots of room. About an hour out of Salzburg, we noticed a huge crowd on a pier and figured that most people would get off and the crowd on the pier would board. Half right—everyone on the pier boarded, but no one got off. This process kept repeating itself along the river at different towns until we thought that we would capsize. There was standing room only on the boat.

In Munich, we rehearsed at the opera house but played at another theater. The opera house had sustained a direct hit during the war. One day after rehearsal, I opened a fire door, and there below me was the auditorium of the opera house still lying in shambles from a bomb.

We traveled by train from Vienna to Berlin, crossing behind the Iron Curtain, and not being allowed off the train at any of the stops. The train was beautifully decorated with wood paneling, but outside in the fields was a time warp. Horses pulled plows with not a tractor in sight. West Berlin was neat, with war rubble carefully stacked in vacant lots. In East Berlin, on the other hand, the rubble lay where it had fallen. Balanchine and the other Russian-born members of the company flew to Berlin, not wanting to take any chance of getting caught on Russian soil.

The thrill of standing on stage and the curtain rising at the Paris Opera House was electrifying. The labyrinth backstage at the Paris Opera House was mystifying. The receptions at palaces and palazzos and embassies were intoxicating.

The reek of my *Western Symphony* costume was also memorable. After the success of the ballet, costumes and a set had been commissioned. The ballet was usually the closing number, so on closing nights, the costumes were packed wet and dried out at the next stop. By the end of the tour, a bottle of Jean Nate couldn't mask the smell of those costumes.

In Paris, I told the company that I would be leaving at the end of the tour because I planned to stay in Europe—the "living in Europe bug" had bitten me. Unfortunately, when I learned what dancers made in Europe, I decided I'd better go back to the States even if I was still planning to leave the company.

In Copenhagen, I came out of the dressing room and opened a door to a flight of stairs down to the stage. At the bottom of the stairs was Tanaquil LeClerq in her second movement *Bouree Fantasque* costume. She was bent over and holding her back and talking to some girls. She had been suffering a bad back for several days and was obviously talking of her ailment. That was the last time I saw her. When she was not at rehearsal the next day, the rumor started to spread that she was very ill. The company made an announcement, just as we were about to board the boat for Malmo and Stockholm, that Tanny would be staying in Copenhagen. She had the symptoms of polio, but several days had to pass before they were sure. Tanny was not only Balanchine's wife and a spectacular talent, she was also an extremely popular member of the company, so we were a depressed company that took the boat to Malmo to board a train for Stockholm. We left Tanny, her mother, and Balanchine in Copenhagen where they stayed for another six months.

On the train, it was announced that the U.S. Army was flying the new polio vaccine to Stockholm. Most of the company took the shot. In Stockholm, another girl went to the hospital with signs of polio, and again, it turned out to be the virus. After a week in Stockholm, we were tired and depressed, thinking about polio, enduring the gloomy weather, and watching candlelit processions protesting the Suez Canal War.

Maybe this was why a party given in the opera house by the Swedish Ballet turned into one of the most drunken parties I had ever attended. There's a reason the Swedes invented aquavit.

# * Chapter 9 *

Christmas of 1956 was a nervous time. I had bought presents in Europe, so that was not a problem, but I was no longer with the company and didn't have a job, and I had to pay for classes. For a dancer, classes go on whether you have a job or not. They become even more important when you don't have a job, in order to keep in condition. A job keeps you in good shape.

In this era, Broadway had what were known as "booking jams." There were not enough theaters to house all the shows that were being produced. The first rush of shows started rehearsing in the late summer so that they could go on tryout tours for several weeks in Boston, New Haven, Philadelphia, Wilmington, or combinations of such, just in time for an early fall opening. The Shuberts and the independent theater owners booked the most promising shows into their theaters. Some shows took to the road without a New York theater booked, hoping that some of the earlier shows booked into a theater would flop and make that theater available. It was like playing a game of musical chairs. Other shows did not go into production until fall, so there was another rush of shows arriving into New York in the middle of winter.

The most desirable theaters were off Times Square in the West Forties. East of Broadway and further uptown were the less desirable theaters, which usually got shows that were thought to be less promising or received transfers of long running shows on their last legs. Curtain time in those days was eight-thirty, and there were seldom Sunday performances except at the City Center. The 104 bus was called the Broadway Express because at seven o'clock at night it was filled with no-name performers traveling from the Upper West Side where they lived to Times Square where they worked.

For four years with the ballet, I had not been going to auditions and had not built that residue of familiarity that one gets from continuous auditioning. You have to learn to audition—how to present yourself, how to dress, and how to push yourself forward without seeming to be pushy. I had no points going into auditions. Rod Alexander came to my rescue. He was announced as the choreographer for *Shinbone Alley*. I auditioned and got the job. Let me tell you, auditioning for someone you know, who you know likes you, is a lot more comfortable than auditioning for a stranger. I felt, going in, that I had a good chance. And I came out with my first Broadway contract. Of course, rehearsal pay was not full pay, but that was better than previously when one did not get paid at all for rehearsing.

*Shinbone Alley* was a musical version of Don Maquis's *archy and mehitabel* stories, the adventures and love story of a cat and a cockroach as written by the cockroach which had appeared as a serial newspaper column. There were no capital letters because archy couldn't jump on the shift key and a letter key at the same time. A couple of years previously, a record had been produced linking the stories together into a narrative with music by George Kleinsinger and lyrics by Joe Darion. Carol Channing had played mehitabel, and Eddie Brackern had played archy.

The prognosis for the show in the gossip circles was not too hot. Assets included the Kleinsinger music, Eartha Kitt as mehitabel, and Eddie Bracken as archy. Debits were that it was too whimsical and we were having no out of town tryouts, a sign that there wasn't a lot of money behind the show. We were booked at the Broadway Theatre, not one of the desirable ones. Chita Rivera and Tom Poston were signed as the understudies to the two stars. Jacques d'Amboise and Allegra Kent from the ballet, which was on hiatus, were signed as the leading dancers. George Irving and Erik Rhodes were also in the cast along with Cathryn ("Skipper") Damon, a dancer before she became an actress, Reri Grist, before she hit the opera, and Carmen Gutierez, one of the world's perfect women, beautiful, a lady, and a professional. Also, there was a vivacious black dancer named Elizabeth Taylor, also known as Frances E.T. Davis. She had gotten to Broadway before the "real" Elizabeth Taylor, so according to Equity rules, if the "real" Elizabeth Taylor wanted to come to Broadway, she would have had to change her name.

When "Skipper" Damon arrived at the ten o'clock rehearsals, she had obviously been up for hours. Her thin red hair was curled and her makeup applied. After ten minutes of working up a sweat dancing, her hair melted, and she began to look like one of the cats we were supposed to portray. It must have been frustrating to her because in a moment of pique I heard her say of Allegra Kent, "Yes, she's a pretty girl, but why does she have to walk around with her face hanging out?" Allegra could pop out of bed, put a rubber band around her hair, and be ready. Skipper could read Rod's moods, and I learned to take her lead. If Skipper was joking or horsing around, Rod was in a good mood. If Skipper was serious, Rod was in a bad mood, and it was best to mind one's p's and q's. I couldn't read his moods, but by following Skipper, I avoided his wrath being directed towards me.

The usual rehearsal period for a musical was four weeks plus an extra two for the dancers. So, thirty years before *Cats*, we were running around a rehearsal hall pretending to be cats and dogs, plus one cockroach. The director was someone no one had heard of. I think he was head of the drama department at Syracuse University, not a well-known name on Broadway. By the time we opened, he had left the show, so we opened with no directorial credit, although Rod had pretty much taken over by then.

We opened at the Broadway Theatre for four weeks of previews in lieu of an out of town tryout. Normally shows came into New York after a tryout and had one or two previews before opening night. Producers were beginning to have more previews at the regular performance price scale before declaring an "opening," and this process had become a bone of contention between producers and critics. For producers, previews gave them the opportunity to continue working on the show, and it cost them less money than staying out of town. Critics thought the public was being shafted. Personally, I've never understood why newspapers and magazines think they have to protect the public from inferior theatrical products. They don't have the same concern when it comes to new cereals or soap products, but it's tradition. The producers use good notices to sell their product, and damn the critics if the notices aren't good.

Eartha Kitt had a sensational entrance in *Shinbone Alley*. A fire escape was hung just below and upstage of the proscenium with ladders from stage right and left giving access. When the curtain went up, several of us "cats" were on this apparatus, and we started the opening number. I couldn't wait to get off because the fire escape swung back and forth. The extra hazard pay didn't alleviate my fear. After a couple of minutes of singing and dancing about mehitabel, we looked up at Eartha as she walked from right to left across that fire escape with only her legs visible to the audience. What an entrance! She began her opening number half way down the left stage ladder, unfazed by the height or the wobbling.

After the previews, we had our opening night and the reviews were predictable—great for Eartha and Eddie, nice for the music and concept, but not so good for execution. There was no opening party planned, so Eartha gave an impromptu party at her place, the famed "House on 92nd Street" at 160

East Ninety-Second Street. We hung on for about seven weeks, which was normal for a musical unless it was a notorious flop that closed on opening night like *Buttrio Square*. We were not a notorious flop, just an ordinary flop. Maybe if we had been on Forty-Fifth Street and could have picked up some walk-in business, we would have lasted a while longer, but there wasn't much walk-in business up at Fifty-Third and Broadway.

One day I met Mr. Balanchine on the street after he had finally returned from Europe with Tanny, and we stopped to chat. He asked me what I was doing, and I told him I was doing a show. He paused a moment, wrinkled his nose like a chipmunk as he was wont to do, and rubbed his fingers together as he said, "More money." The minimum scale for Actor's Equity was higher than that for the American Guild of Musical Artists that handled ballet.

Closing in late May, the prospects of a new show were not good until late summer. Rod Alexander was again my savior. He was doing a lot of television choreography and almost immediately called me to do the *Arthur Murray Show*, televised from the Ziegfeld Theatre, as well as the *Steve Allen Show*, televised from the old Hudson Theatre. The Hudson, Ziegfeld, and Century Theatres had been turned into television studios. Not only was television siphoning off the theatrical audiences, it was also taking over the work places. I didn't really like performing on television, but it paid more money than Broadway. If you were lucky, there were residuals—payments from rebroadcasts that were a nice surprise when they came in. I never felt part of a television show. TV was like a rehearsal with no payoff, kind of like sex without an orgasm. Even though the shows were live, there was no sense of immediacy and there was even less of that sense later on when shows started to be taped. Once, Ginger Rogers had a boom deliberately dropped into a frame in order to make the show look live. If you were on early in the program, you could be home in time to watch the end of the show on your own television set. There were no bows and no applause, but I never refused a job because anytime I was working I was content.

In one number on the *Arthur Murray Show*, I ended the number kneeling and my partner would throw herself into a pose over my knee. During the camera rehearsal, she threw herself with such force that she hit her head on the stage with such a resounding thud that Kathryn Murray, who was in the sound booth, came rushing out to find out if the girl was alright. She was OK. She just had a nice goose egg on her head, but for a few minutes I thought I had maimed her.

Eight years after leaving high school on my way to Broadway, I had finally made it. I'd been sidetracked by ballet, gone around the world, done two European tours, traveled the United States, done revivals of musicals, and I had been in a Broadway show. I now had my name in Daniel Blum's *Theatre World*, an annual book listing the shows that had been on Broadway and on the road that year. It's a nice ego boost at first, but after a few years, it tends to backhand you when people say, "I was looking through an old *Theatre World* last night. I didn't know you were in that. I had no idea you were that old." It's interesting how some people suddenly drop five years out of his or her life thinking no one will notice.

# * Chapter 10 *

---

*I* n early June 1957, I auditioned for a new musical about the street gangs of New York. Street gangs were a big social worry at that time, and the papers were full of stories about gangs fighting over turf. Gang murders like the famous Umbrella Man murder made headlines. This show was taking the gang situation and loosely overlaying it with *Romeo & Juliet* with the Montagues and the Capulets being the Sharks and the Jets. It didn't sound like my kind of show, but Jerome Robbins was doing the choreography, Leonard Bernstein was doing the music, Stephen Sondheim was doing the lyrics, Irene Sharaff was doing the costumes, Jean Rosenthall was doing the lights, and the book was by Arthur Laurents. It was being produced by Hal Prince, Bobby Griffith, and Freddie Brisson, Rosalind Russell's husband. Obviously, the big guns of Broadway were connected to this show. It had all the earmarks of a hit, or at least it had a good chance of being one. Having worked with Jerry at the ballet, I thought I might have one step up on the ladder.

At the audition, Jerry looked at me and said that I looked familiar. After all those hours rehearsing *The Concert* with him as well as having danced in other ballets of his that he had obviously seen, I didn't seem to have made a big impression on him. Or was this his way of putting me down and telling me

I had no special standing at this audition? I was called back to the final audition and was told to be prepared to sing a song. That was panic time for me because the idea of singing by myself to a darkened auditorium terrified me. A friend told me to sing "Steppin' Out with My Baby" because it was, except for the bridge, one note. I sang it but I didn't make the final cut, although I think it was not because of my one note song. I was disappointed because it was a Jerome Robbins's show and I would have liked to do it.

A couple of nights later, Ruth Mitchell, the stage manager, called and said that Jerry had changed his mind and wanted me in the show, but he wasn't certain whether I was to "swing" the show or be one of the gang members. To "swing" a show means that you are the general understudy for the ensemble. My options were to continue working with Rod for more money on television, which I didn't really enjoy, or to take the job being offered, or to wait and see if I could get another show. I'm basically cautious and decided that "a bird in the hand..." and accepted the job.

I understand that the show was originally called *East Side Story*," but *East Side* in New York connotes rich, not what this story was about. The name was temporarily *Gangway*, which was the name stenciled on the sets. By the time rehearsals began, it had become *West Side Story*.

Because there was to be so much dancing in the show, and because Jerry was doing the choreography with Peter Genarro as co-choreographer, Actor's Equity had given special dispensation for an extra two weeks of rehearsal for the dancers. Therefore, the dancers would work for four weeks before the principals were to begin rehearsing.

Those principals were not well-known names. Chita Rivera had done several shows and had earned a slight name, but mostly she was known just in the business. Larry Kert was even less known. Carol Lawrence had done a couple of shows, including *New Faces of 1952* and an unsuccessful *Ziegfeld Follies* where

Walter Kerr, the critic, had said "watch this girl," but she was hardly a big name. The "money" names were Arthur Laurents, Leonard Bernstein, and Jerome Robbins, whose billing had a box around his name. A box around your name was the new elitist billing for directors, so their names would not be lost among the credits.

In late June, all the dancers gathered at Chester Hale's studio on West Fifty-Sixth Street next to Carnegie Hall, and the production of *West Side Story* began. Jerry had an assistant, Howard Jeffrey, and Peter had an assistant, Wallace Seibert. It was immediately impressed upon us that there would be no chorus in this show, even though at this point most of us were unidentified by a character name. We were all to be distinct personalities. An announcement was made that there were to be no more haircuts for the boys. Great, I was losing my hair, and we were all to let our hair and sideburns grow. The idea of my swinging the show seemed to have disappeared. Now, I was a member of the Sharks, the Puerto Rican gang of Latins and Blacks—the swarthy ones. The other gang was the Jets, the blonds and lighter skinned dancers. Jerry started staging the opening number with the now famous "snap, snap, snap."

It was quite a group. Reri Grist, Elizabeth Taylor, David Winters, and Carmen Gutierrez came from *Shinbone Alley*. Lee Becker Theodore and Liane Plane came from the ballet. Grover Dale, Martin Charnin, and Tony Mordente were later to carve out careers as writers or directors. Ronnie Lee later became one of the biggest theater party brokers.

Rehearsals with Jerome Robbins were intense. He came prepared to work and expected his company to do the same. He knew where he was and where he wanted to go. He didn't always know how to get from point A to point B, so, therefore, he experimented a great deal and frequently had several versions of the same number that he then mixed and matched. He was demanding at one moment and joking the next. His moods were difficult to read with the result that everyone was on edge most of the time. There was no official edict, but the Jets and the Sharks kept to themselves most of the time, and a slight enmity developed between the two gangs. The gangs tended to lunch and socialize only with members of their own gang. I think that this was encouraged because it created a more conflicted feeling between the gangs that played well onstage.

When it was time to set the dance at the gymnasium/dance hall—the famous rumble which was a competition between the two gangs—we separated into different studios. In addition to Chester Hale's studio, we rehearsed at the Broadway Theatre, as well as the Anta and the 54th Street Theatres. The music for the competition had been marked off for the Jets, the Sharks, and everyone else. Peter Gennaro, the lost man in all of this, took the Sharks and choreographed their sections while Jerry worked with the Jets. We didn't know what the other group was doing until we put the number together in one studio. Then Jerry melded and edited the two groups into one another.

I say that Peter was the lost man in all of this because, I think, he had never been given his due in the creation of *West Side Story*. The entire "America" number was his, and a great deal of the style of the dance hall section and the steps of the Sharks were his. Peter was out of the Dunham School of dance, and therefore, he had a lot of ethnicity in his steps and style. I'm certainly not trying to downgrade Jerry—he earned his reputation, but Peter's contribution to *West Side Story* was significant.

Jerry asked some of us to stay late and work at night. We worked on the second act ballet, and it was the nicest rehearsal I had during the show. There was no tension, just relaxed work, which of course is when ballet works best. At the end of the evening, Jerry said, "Nice work." Wow, a compliment from Jerry! The ballet was done on a bare stage with a backdrop, all light, space, and air. At the end of the ballet, the sets came back on stage with the intent of being crushing and oppressive. They didn't get the desired effect until one night, during technical rehearsals, the stage manager inadvertently left the work light on in the flies, which created menacing shadows as the sets came back on stage. Sometimes the best things happen by accident.

After four weeks of rehearsals, we left Chester Hale's studio and moved into the Broadway Theatre to rehearse with the principals. We rehearsed the music in the lounge, and the scenes and dances on the stage or on stages in other theaters. If there was nothing else to do, we were sent to the lounge to do improvisations. It was eight weeks of sore muscles, bruised egos, and sweating bodies in the heat of a New York summer. Jerry frequently seemed to be riding someone in particular, and it was embarrassing to the rest of the cast. We were embarrassed for the object of his displeasure, and at the same time, glad that it was not one of us. The next day we would be relieved that his bad humor hadn't turned elsewhere. Yet, during a break or a lunch hour, Jerry might be found telling jokes in a corner. One never knew in what humor he would be and when it might change. I was not very happy in the show, and one day I told Jerry that I would like out. He told me I was needed, and wanted, and important, and blah, blah, blah…the usual ego booster conversation. It worked and I decided to stay. A couple of days later, all of us who did not have character names were given character names. Mine was "Anxious." Was there a connection between wanting out of the show and my new name? I didn't know, but Jerry was always good with nicknames.

There was a growing tradition of musicals giving a "gypsy" run through before going out of town on a tryout tour. "Gypsy" is Broadway parlance for chorus dancers. The gypsy show was the first chance producers had of seeing the show in front of an audience. It was a friendly audience made up of other performers invited via notices posted backstage at all the current shows. The run through was done in practice clothes with chairs and benches being placed around the stage as sets, and using only work lights. Ours was done at a packed Broadway Theatre, and at the end of the show, the audience sat there stunned. The word went out that the show was something to be reckoned with. Words like "great," "the best," and "innovative" were used to describe the show. Everyone said we couldn't miss, and that we would be the season's great hit. At the end of the gypsy run through, Lauren Bacall just sat in her seat with tears in her eyes.

We went to the National Theatre in Washington, D.C., for out of town tryouts. Equity had won its battle and the National was now desegregated. Once you were out of town, under union rules, you could rehearse five hours a day plus give a performance with only one day a month totally free. We used all of it. We saw the sets for the first time, adjusted ourselves to the sets, wore the costumes for the first time, and heard orchestrations for the first time. Leonard Bernstein's music was sensational. We opened to good notices and spent a few hours relaxing after the show at the Variety Club in the Willard Hotel. We were feeling pretty good about ourselves.

The "Rumble" number was choreographed to a degree, but there was also a lot of free form improvisation in it, so if someone decided to do something different, someone else was apt to get an elbow in the eye. One night, Carol Lawrence pounded on Larry Kert's chest so hard while screaming, "Killer, Killer, Killer" that he had his chest taped for weeks. Voices became husky and disappeared from overuse. Scenes were moved from the first act to the second, and then back again and vice versa. Dance steps were added, and dance steps were subtracted. Minor changes and major changes were made, and all were designed to make the show play better.

When we closed in Washington, we moved north to the Erlanger Theatre in Philadelphia where the process continued. One night after the show, I ran into a very frustrated Lee Becker Theodore outside the Variety Club at the Bellevue-Stratford Hotel. I had been a sometime confidante of Lee's since our Slavenska-Franklin days. She said that Jerry had asked her to marry him. We talked and my advice was, "Don't." She wandered away, and I never heard another word, not even a rumor, about it. I was curious, but Lee never brought the subject up again and trusted that I wouldn't say anything. And, I haven't, until now.

*West Side Story* created a lot of excitement back in New York while we were out of town. One day in Philadelphia, Sammy Davis, Jr., came to see a matinee performance and immediately invited the cast to dinner between shows. Shortly after we opened in New York, Jerry Lewis did the same thing when he saw a matinee.

Over the years, the "gypsy robe" tradition had grown. It started in *Gentlemen Prefer Blondes*. In the chorus of that show were two dancers, Bill Bradley and Arthur Partington. Arthur was forever teasing Bill about his dirty, ragged theater robe. Arthur eventually left the cast to do *Call Me Madam*, and on opening night, he received a package from Bill. It was Bill's old robe with a note of "good luck." The tradition was born. On the next opening of a musical, Arthur sent the robe to a friend in the cast but with a memento from *Call Me Madam* attached. Ever since then, the recipient would attach a memento from the current show and send it to a chorus member of the new show. Other traditions, such as kissing all the cast members while wearing the robe or walking around the stage in the robe before the first curtain, had grown as well. I don't remember who received the robe in *Shinbone Alley*. My first memory of it was from *West Side Story*. Elizabeth Taylor was the recipient, and by that time the robe was heavy with souvenirs from so many shows over the years. Eventually, Actor's Equity took possession of it and created a new robe for the tradition. By now there have probably been several incarnations of the robe. It's supposed to be given only to chorus members, but the tradition has been bent a bit. Tallulah Bankhead received it for *Ziegfeld Follies*, and she was hardly a gypsy.

On September 26, 1957, we opened *West Side Story* at the Winter Garden Theatre at Fiftieth Street and Broadway. It was a hit. Not a huge hit on the order of *My Fair Lady* that we had been hoping for and thought it deserved, but a hit nonetheless. Bernstein conducted the opening, and the glamorous people of New York were in attendance. Coming down the stairs from the dressing rooms to the stage level after the premiere, I bumped into Tyrone Power with Marlene Dietrich on his arm.

It was nice to be in a hit show. Somehow it made you walk a little taller. There was admiration in the eyes of people who told you how much they liked the show. A lot of people hinted, sometimes not so subtly, that they would like you to get them tickets to the Actor's Fund performance. All shows, per union contract, gave an extra Sunday night performance to benefit the Actor's Fund. These performances were the only chance that other actors who were working in other Broadway shows had to see the concurrently running shows. Knowing that the audience was comprised largely of other performers, these performances were expected to be special, and everyone gave their best. Tickets to these performances were hard to secure. This had become a social event and the place to be seen. I gave one of my allotted tickets to Virginia Lee and saved the other for Mom, who was coming to New York for the performance.

Mom was easy to entertain in New York. All I had to do was set her down in the window seat of the Times Square Automat with a cup of coffee, and she was content to people watch for hours. Mom had seen me perform with the ballet in various cities, but this was the first time she saw her kid on Broadway.

News of the show spread to some unlikely places, and after one matinee, some of the cast were met outside the stage door by a real gang and challenged to a rumble. It was explained that we were not real gangs, only theatrical ones, but for a while, there was some unease that we might be having a rumble after the show.

I made my first movie as a result of *West Side Story*. An audition notice was posted backstage for a dance in a nightclub scene. It sounded like fun to me as well as an extra paycheck, so I went to the audition at a soundstage in the Bronx and was

cast as an extra in the movie, *The Pusher.* For the next several
months, I watched Variety for news of its release. I never saw or
heard anything about it until several years later. Crossing Forty-
Second Street and Broadway, I looked down the street at all the
marquees of the second run theaters and there was *The Pusher.*
I changed all my plans and went to see it. I saw my face on the
silver screen for about two seconds. The movie was pretty bad.

During a rehearsal one day, Jerry looked at me and asked,
"How long are you going to stay with the show?"

I don't remember if I said or only thought, "Does that mean
you want me to leave?" Whichever, things were churning.
I had never been very content in the show, and I was in the
middle of a major romance that was turning sour. I was breast-
beating for all it was worth, and it probably had affected my
performances. A change of scenery was on my mind.

Shortly after *West Side Story* opened, the cast was invited
to a gypsy run through of a new musical, *The Music Man*, with
Robert Preston and Barbara Cook at the Ethel Barrymore
Theatre. I went and left after the first act. I didn't like it, but
then there wasn't much I liked with my romance on the rocks. A
couple of months later, *The Music Man* opened to rave reviews.
The next night George Marcy walked into the dressing room
and said, "There goes the Tony Award." He was right. Months
later, *West Side Story* joined the distinguished company of major
achievements that did not win the Tony.

Carol Lawrence had gotten to appear on the *Ed Sullivan
Show*, and afterwards, she started to receive applause immediately
as she made her entrance every night. *West Side Story* had not
made her a star, but Ed Sullivan was doing it. Soon, it was
difficult to turn the television to any variety show and not see
Carol. Carol had become "Miss Television." Walter Kerr had
been right when he said, "Watch this girl." She was not a great
dancer, but I must say, I never saw the woman hit a bad line.

The year 1958 was approaching, and there was to be a
World's Fair in Brussels. In the trade papers, I noticed an

audition for a group that was to perform at the World's Fair. With my busted romance on my mind, I wanted to escape to Europe, so I auditioned and got the job. I didn't know whether or not to quit *West Side Story*, but I had some time before I had to make a decision.

At the same time, rumors started floating that Jerry was forming a company that would open at the new Spoleto Festival. Another rumor started floating that Jerry was going to take some dancers from *West Side Story* for the Spoleto company. One matinee day, the day before I had to sign a contract for the World's Fair job, the stage manager told me to go home between shows because Jerry was going to call me about the Spoleto company. I went home after the matinee, and I waited, but there was no call. There was no call at the theater that night either. Nothing was ever said. Annoyed at what I thought was shabby treatment, I turned in my notice to *West Side Story*, and I signed a contract to go to the World's Fair in Brussels.

# * Chapter 11 *

Six of us, three men and three women, met at the airlines terminal on First Avenue and Thirty-Eighth Street late on a snowy Sunday afternoon for the trip to Paris. We were to be joined in Paris by an English dancer for a month of rehearsals before going on to Brussels. We arrived at Idlewild in good time for a 6 p.m. flight, but, as it turned out, there was no hurry. The snowstorm had disrupted all the flights, and we didn't board until 9 p.m. Then there was a bomb scare, and we had to get off the flight. All of our luggage had to be offloaded, checked, and reloaded. Finally, around midnight, we took off for Paris, had dinner, and fell asleep. A few hours later, I awoke. Curtis Hood, who was sitting next to me, said, "Strange, we're going West."

I thought, "Curtis, learn your geography. Europe is *east* of North America." Luckily, I didn't say it but checked the sun's position instead. Curtis was right; we were going West. Shortly, everyone awoke when the captain announced that we were about to land at Idlewild. We had flown almost to the point of no return when the number one engine had gone out, and we had had to turn around.

Back on land at Idlewild, we heard announcements every hour that the flight had been delayed again. Free food was available, although the selection was getting small because there were no deliveries to the airport that day due to the snowstorm. We heard that the brakes of the airplane were freezing. Finally, about three in the afternoon, we boarded our plane again. As we sped down the runway, the number four engine went out, so we taxied back to the terminal. Ultimately, we took off in the wee hours and finally made it to Paris early Tuesday evening. It had taken almost two days to fly to Paris. Looking back, it was a bad omen.

We settled into Paris for rehearsals. I stayed at the Hotel Mont Joli on Rue Fromentin. Valerie Camille, an American who had trained with Jack Cole, had hired us, and therefore our act was to be ersatz Cole. The vicious rumor was that Valerie worked in Europe because she was afraid of being compared to Gwen Verdon if she returned to the States. Valerie was fun and a good dancer, but Gwen Verdon she was not. Valerie had a relationship with her producer, Andre Pousse, who supposedly had been a champion bicycle rider and a former lover of Edith Piaf.

Valerie was a redhead as were two of the other girls in the company. One of the girls, Lynn, had the most gloriously natural red hair I had ever seen. The other redhead, Marcia, decided that there were too many red heads and that she would become platinum blonde. She had her hair stripped, and it came out many hued from platinum to a tinge of pink. Not having makeup for a platinum blonde, she tried to mix her makeup. When I passed her on the way to rehearsal one morning, she looked like a fifty-year-old who had been working the streets all night. Eventually, with more stripping and new makeup, she looked fine. Several years later she went back to her original brunette and looked sensational.

Valerie, like all Cole-trained dancers, was disciplined and determined. She choreographed one number in which she did several steps on a platform a couple of feet higher than the stage. In rehearsals, she used a bench with wobbly legs to represent the platform. Every time she got on the bench, it tipped and threw her off, but she refused to recognize that the uneven legs were the problem, not her technique. Every day we watched her fall off the bench, stop the rehearsal, and take it from the beginning, only to fall off the bench again. Her determination was comical and admirable and rather typical of dancers who refuse to admit defeat.

After rehearsals, we socialized with expatriate American dancers who were in Europe for one reason or another. Don Lurio was there trying to get started as a choreographer, and several dancers were working with George Rich in his small ballet company, Ballet Ho. I thought that one of the girls in his company, Nicole Coissille, was an American who spoke French because she spoke idiomatic English, but I later discovered she had learned English by hanging out with American dancers. Unfortunately, a couple of the dancers had lisps, and Nicole spoke English with a lisp. Years later, she turned up singing the title song on the soundtrack of the movie, *A Man and A Woman*.

There was a dancer named Lenny in the company who was a spectacular jazz dancer and had an egocentric personality. I've forgotten his last name, but I do remember that Lenny's obsession was his derriere. Walking down the street with Lenny was an experience. He always wanted you to check the people behind us to see if they were looking at his ass. He thought that no one could ignore his rump and that all who saw it were admiring it. He and a couple of the girls had had death masks made at a bar. Their faces were greased, straws stuck up their nostrils, and then their faces were covered with plaster to make a mold. Their masks turned out very well, and the next night, Lenny went to have his butt immortalized. I don't know if they used any straws.

After a month of rehearsals, we departed for Brussels where we stayed on a barge in a canal. We each had a small room, and there was a dining room on the barge for meals. Our first dinner was a nice chicken stew. At least I thought it was chicken until I noticed that the leg joint turned the wrong way. It was rabbit. The barge was kind of romantic for the first couple of days. We all went out and bought fabric to make curtains for our little monk cells. The romanticism paled a bit after a few days as we looked out our portholes at the sewage floating by.

We were to perform in an arena in the honky-tonk amusement section of the fair that was set off in one corner far from the Atomium and the national exhibits. The star attraction was the Charlivels family of acrobats and singers consisting of a father and three sons. Another part of the show was an American aquacade. The arena had a pool with a retractable cover that was opened for the aquacade and became a stage when it was closed. There were also to be guest artists from time to time. It all turned out to be quite dreary. The arena sat about two thousand customers, but we seldom had more than a couple of hundred. It was always dank because of the pool. I remember only one guest artist, Annie Corde. This was April, and the big crowds were not expected until summer when the tourists arrived.

The barge became less and less romantic, so we all rented rooms closer to the Exposition. I bought a bicycle, which allowed me to get around. I also bought a hot plate for my room. It kept blowing the fuses. It all started to be rather depressing, and I felt like I was in the dregs of "show biz." I gave up *West Side Story* for this dismal tour? What had I been thinking?

After a few weeks of almost no business, the aquacade pulled out of the show, and we closed for a couple of weeks to reorganize. I used the free time to take a train to Spoleto where Buzz Miller was working with John Butler. I thought a surprise visit would be fun. I shared a compartment on the train with an Italian soldier, another man, and a small old lady. The Italian soldier spent most of the trip asleep with an enormous erection bulging in his pants. I spent my time staring at it, then checking to see if anyone was watching me. When I looked at the other man, he was also staring at the Italian boner, and then looking to see if I had noticed him watching. The little old lady self-consciously stared at the corridor.

One should know better than to surprise people. When I arrived in Spoleto, Buzz, who was sharing a house with Glen Tetley, was away exploring Umbria. The Butler Dance Company had the day off, so I couldn't find anyone I knew. I walked around Spoleto until evening when Buzz and Glen returned. They gave me a place to sleep, and we had breakfast together in the morning. After, I got back on the train for Rome and Paris. No one was showing his national colors on the return trip.

Back in Brussels, we reopened the show. Business did not improve, although socially it was more fun because the State Department was sending American musicals as part of the United States contribution to the World's Fair. *Carousel* and *Wonderful Town* were performed at the American Pavilion, so there were a good many American dancers in town with whom to socialize. Other friends making European tours and stopping at the fair visited. Our show, however, was going straight down the drain. Lenny had already left and had been replaced, although nothing could replace Lenny's legendary ass. It was time to turn in my notice.

I returned to Paris to book passage home. The Hotel Mont Joli was full, so I checked into a hotel around the corner. That night while I was sleeping, a bullet came through the window and lodged in the wall above my head. The Corsicans were acting up again. I wanted to go home by ship because I had never crossed the ocean by ship. I found cabin class passage on the *Queen Mary* and was ready to leave when the telephone rang. George Reich was on the phone asking me to join his company, Ballet Ho, which was really tempting and one of the things I had on my mind. However, when I learned how much the salary was, I decided to return to New York. I didn't know how those dancers survived on the salaries they were earning. I had no idea how George knew I was back in Paris or how he found out at which hotel I was staying. George lived with the actor, Jean Marais. The company had all spent a day as his guests in their home outside Paris. It was filled with mementoes of Sartre and Picasso. I could have survived very well for the rest of my life living in the pool house.

I took the boat train to London in order to visit Kay Sargeant from the New York City Ballet. She had married the head electrician at Covent Garden and moved to England. After London, it was on to Southampton and the *Queen Mary*. We sailed on a beautiful day in late July, and I took the sun on the way to Le Havre. Then we sailed into a fog bank and didn't emerge from it until we got to New York. It seemed a fitting metaphor for this European misadventure.

# * Chapter 12 *

This was the second time I was coming home from
Europe without a job, but I emerged into sunlight
despite the fog that had spoiled my crossing. Jerome
Robbins's new project, *Ballets: U.S.A.*, had been a big hit in
Spoleto and returned to the States about the same time I did.
Because of its success at Spoleto, it was quickly booked for a
two-week New York engagement. Shortly after I arrived home,
I received a call from Jerry's representative asking me to join
*Ballets: U.S.A.* I didn't hesitate in accepting. I whooped and
danced around my apartment as soon as I hung up the phone.

For the New York engagement, Jerry was creating a
curtain opener entitled *3 X 3* to join his *New York Export,
Opus Jazz*, *Afternoon of A Faun*, and *The Concert*. The company
included Todd Bolender, Wilma Curly, and John Mandia from
New York City Ballet, as well as Maria Karnilova from Ballet
Theatre and numerous other shows. Jay Norman from *West
Side Story* and Pat Dunn from the Jack Cole company also
joined. I had been in on the creation of *The Concert* at New
York City Ballet, so it was familiar to me. *New York Export
Opus Jazz* was to be the *pièce de résistance*. It was completely
new to me, and I had to learn it. On the first day of rehearsal,
Jerry started *3 X 3* and cast me as one of the three couples.
After devising about three steps, he did his "Jerry" thing—he

looked in my direction and said, "You'd better learn this." This was not a confidence booster for me, but it was the way Jerry worked.

All dancers admired and respected Jerry's talent, but there were also many who at one time or another would have liked to use a shiv on him. There is a story about Jerry that I have heard many times but have no idea whether it is true or not. It may only be wishful thinking based on something that could have happened. Supposedly during the out of town tryout of a musical, he was giving notes to the cast on stage after a performance. He was saying something like, "And if you ever do that again...," as he backed away from the cast towards the edge of the stage. They let him fall backwards into the orchestra pit. Fortunately, he suffered no serious injuries and went on to even greater success.

*Ballets: U.S.A.* opened at the Alvin Theatre on Fifty-Second Street on September 4, 1958, to great reviews. Business was exceptional enough that we were extended for three extra weeks. It was also decided to send the company on a national tour. The dilemma Jerry faced was whether to send us out immediately or wait six months and generate publicity for the tour. Because Jerry was about to start the movie version of *West Side Story*, he decided to send us out immediately. Bad decision. We received glowing notices everywhere but did bad business. We closed in Cleveland within sight of Christmas.

During rehearsals for *Ballets: U.S.A.*, I had to take care of a growing problem. Actually, the problem, my hair, was just the opposite of a growing problem because my baldness was expanding, and my self-consciousness about it was growing even faster. So, I gritted my teeth and went to a wig maker to order a toupee. The trauma of having the top of my head shaved was offset by the result, which turned out nicely. The toupee was set in among the rest of my hair and looked pretty decent. At least I felt better with a new head of hair, a new nose, and a new name. I'd also spent a lot of time in the gym and had a pretty good new torso. The dancing had reformed and developed my legs. There wasn't a lot left of the eighteen-year-old kid who had left Brown City for New York.

One experience on the tour of *Ballets: U.S.A.* is etched in my memory. We were playing at the American Theatre in St. Louis. One day, three of us, including John Jones, a black dancer, walked into the Chinese restaurant next to the theater. A Chinese maitre d' met us at the door and quietly informed us that the restaurant didn't serve "colored people." We were so stunned that we sheepishly backed out of the restaurant before realizing the irony of a Chinese man saying they didn't serve colored people. I'm ashamed that I didn't create a scene by throwing the cash register through the window or calling the ACLU or something, but I didn't, and it probably would not have done any good except to absolve my conscience a bit. Imagine it, 1958, and the Chinese restaurant right next door to the American Theatre would not serve African-Americans. When we went to Miami for a week, John Jones emerged from his hotel room only for performances. He would be taking no more chances on another racial incident.

When *Ballets: U.S.A.* closed, we all received a letter from the management saying they were sorry, but after Jerry got the movie of *West Side Story* out of the way, the company would reform. I was filling in with the occasional television show when a spot opened up in *West Side Story*—at least until summer when the show was to go on tour. It was preproduction work for the movie version, but there was no chance of my being in the movie. I was too old by now and wearing a toupee. I simply didn't look like a teenage gang member anymore, but it was fun and interesting to do some of the preproduction work. We scouted locations on the West Side of Manhattan, and we performed some of the numbers in these locations, one of which was a playground on West Forty-Fifth Street where the Capeman and Umbrella Man murders had taken place.

Jerry gave a party for the *Ballets: U.S.A.* company and some of the cast from *West Side Story*. He gave me what I think was a backhanded compliment. The costumes for *The Concert* were blue union suits worn with attached collars, ties, and hose with garters. The effect was rather nerdish. At his house, I was looking at a sketch of the costume hanging on his wall. He came up to me, looked at the sketch, and said, "You're the only one who doesn't look nude in that costume." I think he was telling me that I had a good body, but the backhanded part was that the intent of the costume was that we would look nude, and I had thwarted the intention.

*West Side Story* closed in New York to go on tour. *Ballets: U.S.A.* was reformed to go back to Spoleto, and then do a brief European tour. When I went to Leland Hayward's office to sign the contract, I discovered that the original members of the company were to receive a higher salary than either I or any new members were to be paid. Maybe this was fair, or maybe it wasn't, but it put my nose out of joint again, and I decided not to go with them. Pride can really get in one's way, although this time it worked out just fine. There were, however, some repercussions later on.

I was out of work, but I did have a new apartment. The apartment in the front of the building where I was living had become vacant, and the landlord said I could have it which meant that I knew of an available rent controlled apartment, my old one. Everyone always wanted a rent controlled apartment, so I spread the word that one was available. Wouldn't you know, no one I knew was in the market for a new apartment then. Finally, an actor friend sent an unemployed actor over to look at the apartment, and he said he wanted it. I gave him the landlord's number and put in a good word with the landlord. He moved in, and within two weeks, he was burglarized. Within six months, his girlfriend left him. Nothing was working for him, including gainful work as an actor. As the saying goes, "He couldn't get arrested." A couple of years later, I met him in the hallway, and he said he was going to California to see if things would be better out there. About a year later, I turned on the television, and there he was, Harvey Korman, playing second banana to Danny Kaye.

Besides Broadway, television, summer stock, and industrial shows were sources of income for dancers. Industrial shows were entertainments presented by companies for their sales people at which they presented new products and created an atmosphere of boosterism. The most prestigious of the shows was the Oldsmobile Show. The Oldsmobile production people either wrote a new musical around old music or adapted an old show to their purposes. The previous year they had used *Good News* and instead of the star football player having to pass his French class, in this version, he had to pass his class in salesmanship. Silly, but it worked. The stars of the show were Florence Henderson, Bill Hayes, and the next year's Oldsmobiles that were revealed during the show. They even spent time in a studio recording the show. Henderson and Hayes were both attractive personalities with good voices and a light touch when delivering the product spiel. However, Carol Haney, who did the choreography and musical staging, was the real star of the show.

Carol had been a contract dancer in the Hollywood musicals and had done a sensational number with Bob Fosse in *Kiss Me Kate*. When Fosse did the dances for *Pajama Game*, he brought Carol with him, and she played the second comic lead. She became an overnight star. Right after the opening, however, she sprained her ankle and was out of the show for a couple of weeks, so her understudy, an unknown named Shirley Maclaine, took over. Shirley was discovered by Hollywood and the rest, as they say, is history.

Carol's assistant on the show was Hugh Lambert who later married Nancy Sinatra. Hugh was an adequate dancer, at best, but he had other attributes of a good chorus person. He was tall, good looking, and looked great standing next to a star. One day while rehearsing for a Bob Alton show, Hugh's ineptitude was frustrating Mr. Alton during a number in which the dancers filled the stage and suddenly split in two, moving to opposite sides of the stage. Hugh forgot the steps and was left standing alone in the middle of the stage. Mr. Alton stopped the rehearsal and asked, "Hugh, which side are you on?" After a couple of embarrassing seconds, Hugh answered, "Your side." He saved his job, and became one of Alton's favorites.

Carol always worked with Luther Henderson who is a minor genius as far as I'm concerned. Carol did the choreography; Luther did the dance music and arrangements. As long as Carol was doing good work, Luther sat at the piano churning out wonderful music. However, if Carol started doing something banal or wrong, Luther would give her lousy, uninspiring music to work with until she turned in the right direction.

After turning down *Ballets: U.S.A.,* I auditioned for Carol Haney and the Oldsmobile Show and was accepted. It was the first of several years where I would work with Carol. The show was presented at the Winter Garden Theatre for a week, and then went to Lansing, Michigan to the Oldsmobile headquarters. The pay scale for industrials was two hundred fifty dollars per week plus per diem when away from New York. After the ten-week contract, I realized that without trying I had saved a thousand dollars—a lot of money to me at that time. During the Oldsmobile Show the following year, I tried to save and did much better than a thousand.

After the Oldsmobile Show, I filled in with television. I particularly enjoyed doing the *Phil Silvers Show.* We did one number on the Staten Island ferry in New York Harbor that was great fun. However, I was looking for a show with a steady income rather than erratic television work. A musical version of *Pride and Prejudice* with choreography by Bobby Hamilton was announced. Bobby had had success on television with his Hamilton Trio that consisted of himself, his wife, Gloria Stevens Hamilton, and Patricia Horn. I went to the audition and was dismissed with the first group. Later in the day, I ran into Gloria and complained that her husband had thrown me out.

She looked stunned for a moment and then started laughing. She then told me that every time Bobby saw me on television, he would point me out and say, "That's a dancer!"

Gloria Stevens Hamilton was a tall dancer with long dark hair and a wonderful sense of humor. Once on Arthur Godfrey's show, Mr. Godfrey asked her and another dancer to sit beside him while he did the commercial for a shampoo. After he finished the commercial, he turned to Gloria and commented, "Gloria, you have such lovely hair. How do you care for it?" Gloria responded, "Oh, I take it off and scrub it on a washboard." She immediately became a favorite of Mr. Godfrey's.

# * Chapter 13 *

*S*aratoga, my next show, looked impressive on paper but didn't amount to much. It was based on the Edna Ferber novel *Saratoga Trunk*, which had been made into a movie starring Ingrid Bergman and Gary Cooper. For the Broadway version, the novel was adapted and directed by Morton DeCosta, with music and lyrics by Harold Arlen and Johnny Mercer, sets and costumes by Cecil Beaton, and lighting by Jean Rosenthal. The stars were Howard Keel who was returning to Broadway, and Carol Lawrence who, after *West Side Story* and her constant television exposure, was a good bet to become a real star. In addition, featured in the show were Carol Brice, the black contralto singer, and Odette Myrtil, a star of the old operettas. One of the chorus women was Virginia Capers who would later win a Tony for the musical version of *Raisin in The Sun*. The choreographer was Ralph Beaumont, and it was his first big show.

We rehearsed the show downtown on Second Avenue. This meant lots of chicken soup and onion rolls for lunch. The most memorable part of the rehearsals was the costume parade. Costume parades are when all of the costumes are shown *en masse* for the first time. Usually shows don't have or won't take the time for the costume parade. But *Saratoga* did and it was spectacular because Cecil Beaton's costumes were gorgeous.

Every time someone appeared in a new costume, there was applause with oohs and ahhs from the cast.

We went to the Shubert Theatre in Philadelphia for our tryout, and it was pretty much a mess. The sets were complicated with both a turntable and a treadmill. Nothing seemed to work at first, which was par for the course. I was in the auditorium one afternoon watching a scene change as one thing after another went wrong. I turned to Jean Rosenthal who was trying to light the show and asked, "Have you ever seen anything like this?" She looked at me and responded, "It's pretty wild, isn't it?" Nothing really upset Jean; she took it as it came and worked with it. Another time while rehearsing a scene, Carol Lawrence was walking on the treadmill wearing a gown with a train. The train caught in the treadmill and was pulling her backwards. As she was about to be strangled, Carol calmly asked, "Could you please stop it?" The woman had nerves of steel.

Philadelphia still had blue laws and was not a fun place to visit unless you knew some locals. Not only did you not want to drink the water, on Sundays you couldn't drink at all except at the Variety Club. Later on, after I had met some Philadelphians, I enjoyed going there. The blue laws forced the populace into sociability, and there were always a lot of private parties to go to on Sundays.

We opened to middling reviews, so the next month we worked with the juxtaposition of old scenes with new scenes, old music with new music, and old lyrics with new lyrics. Like any show that is not a hit out of town, we moved on to New York hoping—but not really believing— that we had improved enough to get good reviews in New York.

One day while there were technical rehearsals at the theater, the cast was rehearsing near Columbus Circle. The dancers weren't needed much, and we were told to take a couple of hours for lunch. It was a beautiful day, and a group of us took our lunches to Central Park to eat. The sun was warm, so a couple of us took our shirts off to enjoy the sun. We had no more than taken our shirts off when a squad car pulled up and gave two of us tickets, telling us to appear in court the next morning. It was embarrassing to have to tell the company that we would be late for rehearsals the next day because we had to go to court.

Early the next morning, I went to court, which was filled with people who had received summonses for littering, not sweeping their sidewalks, and the like. It was subdued bedlam in the court until my name was called and the judge said, "Read the charges."

The clerk, with a much louder voice than he had been using said, "Indecent exposure."

The court suddenly got very quiet. I, the "pervert," had to walk through the courtroom to face the judge. When I got to him, everything was spoken in a low voice. He asked what I had done, and I replied, "Took off my shirt in the park."

"How do you plead?" he asked.

"Guilty."

Then he said "You may be an Apollo to the girls, but keep your shirt on in the park. Two dollars." Then I, the "pervert," had to walk red-faced through the court with everyone staring at me. Nowadays, I often think of this episode when I see all the flesh being exposed on the streets of New York.

We opened in New York on Pearl Harbor Day, 1959, and although the devastation wasn't on a par with Pearl Harbor, we took some direct hits. Obviously, the producers had wasted money painting a huge sign above the Winter Garden Theatre. My only distinct memory of the opening is of Cecil Beaton wearing his Jack Frost hat. He was carrying cans of spray paint and running around touching up the sets just before the curtain rose.

We staggered along until early February, then closed after eighty performances, which was about par for a non-hit musical. We ran long enough to make the cast recording with help from Arlen and Mercer. That recording is probably a collector's item today. The show did have some good music in it. Did Arlen and Mercer ever write any bad music? The sets were burned because storing sets was expensive. Those gorgeous costumes were sold to costume companies and were probably seen in numerous summer stock, television, regional theater, and high school productions of various plays.

*Saratoga* was over, and it was late winter. The only work I found was a revival of *Finian's Rainbow* at the City Center with Jeannie Carson and Biff McGuire. I was rather excited to work with Jeannie Carson. I had seen her in a show in London on my "around the world" trip and was a fan. The cast also included Howard Morris as the leprechaun and Carmen Gutierrez as the mute girl, Susan. Robert Guillame was in the chorus. Howard Morris had one embarrassing night in a scene in which he was divested of his trousers and played the rest of the scene in red long johns. One night he forgot to put on his long johns, and when he lost his trousers, he was on stage in his jock strap. He had to adjust his staging in order not to moon the audience that night.

To our surprise, *Finian's* received glowing notices and immediately there was talk of moving the show to Broadway. There was also talk of an Actor's Equity strike being called. Finally, there was notice that I was not getting any younger. In *Finian's*, I worked with a woman who was the daughter of a woman I had worked with in the Slavenska-Franklin Ballet. It was also almost summer and time for the Oldsmobile Show. Because the Oldsmobile Show paid more, and because if there were to be a strike it wouldn't affect the industrials, and because I loved working with Carol Haney, I chose the Oldsmobile Show rather than continue with *Finian's*.

On the first day of rehearsals for the Oldsmobile Show, Carol announced she was dropping out. She was pregnant and had already had a couple of miscarriages, so she was taking no chances. Hugh Lambert, her assistant, was going to replace her, which he did with great success. Most of his staging was good, but the big number was sensational. It stopped the show every night, and everyone presumed Hugh was on his way to success. However, the company had caught the "bitchiness virus," and it was not a happy company that year. Nice people got caught up in vicious backstabbing done in the name of humor. Some of it was humor and some just plain viciousness. It was one of those situations where you didn't want to leave the room because you knew you'd be the next target if you did. In the end, everyone wound up with hurt feelings.

I did the Oldsmobile Show at the Mark Hellinger Theatre at Fifty-First Street then on the West Coast. *Finian's* moved to the 46th Street Theatre. The actors went on strike, and there was a bit of scandal around the strike vote. By the time the working actors arrived at the Edison Hotel ballroom to vote, the ballroom was filled with non-working actors, so the working actors couldn't get in. Obviously, it was easier to vote to strike when you were not working than when you were.

When the Oldsmobile Show finished on the West Coast, I took a night flight to New York. On the way to my apartment, I stopped at the mailbox and found an announcement that there was an audition for *The Conquering Hero* that morning at 10 a.m. *The Conquering Hero* was the one show that had been announced for the company season that I particularly wanted to do. It was a Bob Fosse show based upon a Preston Sturgis film, *Hail the Conquering Hero.* Fosse was the new "wunderkind" of choreography on Broadway, and I never had worked for him and want to do so.

Sleepless, I packed my dance bag, went to the audition, and felt that I was doing very badly. I had the feeling, however, that Fosse liked me. I did make the first cut and was called back to the final. In the intervening days, I did something I'd never done before and have never done since. I rented a studio and practiced all the steps we had been given at the audition. So, I returned to the final audition thinking that I was well prepared. I danced well, but somewhere during the audition, I got the distinct impression that I was not to be favored. By the end of the audition, we had been whittled down to twelve men and twelve women. Fosse told us that he hadn't yet made his decision and would be in touch. To me that meant that the stage manager might be calling us to say whether we were in or out. I was pretty sure that I was out and a bit depressed by it. That night the phone rang, and there was Bob Fosse on the line apologizing that there didn't seem to be a place for me in the show. I told him that I had gotten that impression during the audition, and he replied, "Gee, you're taking this awfully well." The upshot was that I was disappointed not to be in the show and work for him, but I was terribly impressed that he had taken the time and trouble to call and give me the news personally.

There wasn't much happening on Broadway at that time, so I filled in on some television shows and received unemployment checks. In December, I went to West Palm Beach where a South African ballerina named Johanna had a school and was producing a new ballet at the Royal Poinciana Playhouse. It was an ambitious project. Her students were to make up the ensemble, and she hired some New York dancers to do the leads. Violette Verdy and Michael Maule were the leads along with six other dancers from New York. We were paid room and board plus twenty-five dollars a week. The ballet was pretty bad, but it was a nice vacation for me. I spent Christmas Day —which is also my birthday—at the beach. It was one of the nicest I had ever had with beautiful warm weather, and I had the beach to myself.

After Christmas there still wasn't much happening in New York, and so when the opportunity presented itself, I went to Las Vegas to do the *Jayne Mansfield Show* at the Dunes Hotel. The previous year, Mansfield had been a huge success in Las Vegas in a show staged by Jack Cole. They were going to try again, but this time Jack Cole was not available, so Ethel Martin, who had worked with Jack's company, was hired to stage the show. Ethel asked me to assist her and to be the dance captain. The dance captain was the person who kept the show in shape. Tommy

Wolfe, composer of *Spring Will Really Hang You Up the Most* and *Lush Life*, did special music for the show. The stars were Jayne and her husband, Mickey Hargitay, a body builder and former Mr. USA. I was amused by the idea of working with Mansfield but was not looking forward to Hargitay. Wouldn't you know that he turned out to be a real gentleman who was obviously in love with Jayne. She was really beautiful and didn't have the cheap look she had in her films.

We auditioned dancers and a couple of body builders in Los Angeles, using Mitch Leisen's studio. There were four show girls waiting for us in Las Vegas. The show was called *Jayne's House of Love*. It was based around the theme of Jayne's house. Jayne had bought Rudy Vallee's house in Hollywood, then installed a heart shaped pool and decorated the house totally in pink. Tommy Wolfe wrote some nice material and music, and Ethel did choreography in the style of the time. Ethel was a chic woman, and her staging for Jayne was chic, but by the time Jayne did it, it turned out pretty tawdry. There was nothing subtle about Jayne. She knew what she was selling. We finished rehearsing in Los Angeles, moved to Las Vegas, put the show girls into their numbers, and opened at the Dunes Hotel. It was pretty bad, although everyone agreed that Jayne was so obviously trying to please the audience that the evening ended up being a lot of fun.

This started the worst six weeks of my life. All the dancers hated me. I never knew why—maybe it was a New York versus Los Angeles thing; maybe it was chemistry; maybe we had a different attitude towards work—but there was no doubting the animosity in the air. When the show girls did the first show, then were seen in the Casino socializing with men and not returning for the second show, adjustments had to be made. When I objected to these absences, the alcoholic stage manager told me to shut up or I'd end up in a closet. I began to realize that things were not quite what they seemed. Jayne altered her costumes so that she managed to "accidently" come out of them during performance. One of the chorus boys had some personal trouble and was carrying a pair of brass knuckles in his pocket. I couldn't wait for the six weeks to pass, so I could get out of there. My one amusement was a nickel slot machine that paid off frequently. Several times a day, I would stand by that machine as someone filled it with nickels, and then I would move in to hit jackpot. I was sure the management would eventually notice, but they never said anything to me.

Jayne did one number where she wandered through the audience and sang. One night I was watching from the wing as she sat on a man's lap and sang to him. He had a lit cigarette in his hand and held it very close to her breast. I was horrified, but Jayne held her ground until she was ready to move on. She had guts. I think she also had a lot of talent and could have been much better if she hadn't sunk to the tawdry, but, as I said earlier, she knew what she was selling.

In the fashion of the time, we recorded the show. For two nights, microphones were set up, and we were "live from the Dunes." It took a couple of years for the album to be produced, and when it finally came out, it had been doctored up with additional material from a female impersonator named Arthur Blake. The name of the album was *Jayne Mansfield Busts Up Vegas.* Probably another collector's item.

Near the end of the engagement, salvation, or hopes of it, arrived in the mail. A postcard from *Ballets: USA* arrived, saying that the company was reforming, and asking if I would be interested and available. I wrote back by return mail that I was interested and available. When Jayne's show finally finished, one of the dancers told me never to return to Las Vegas. With thoughts of "that closet" I had been threatened with in mind, I told him I had no intention of coming back. I went to the Sands Hotel to wait until it was time to catch my flight, and I hit a fifteen-dollar jackpot on a dime machine. As I was collecting my coins, I asked a guard which slot machine was due to pay off. He looked at a machine nearby, so I plugged a few dimes into it and hit another jackpot. I tipped the guard and left for the airport.

Back in New York, Jerome Robbins was having classes for the company and for future prospects who might join the company. I had already told Carol Haney that I wouldn't be available for the Oldsmobile Show that year because I was going with *Ballets: USA*, but sometime during those company classes, it dawned on me that I was auditioning again. That postcard had meant exactly what it had said—are you interested and are you available? My relationship with Jerry had always run a little hot and cold. Sometimes he seemed to like me, and at other times, not so much. Nenette Charisse told me that Jerry once said that I made him uncomfortable. I continued to take the company classes until one day at the end of class, Jerry told me to go up to the office and sign my contract. When I got to the office, the company manager seemed confused and embarrassed and said the contract wasn't there yet, maybe tomorrow. I got the message, and that was the end of my association with Jerome Robbins. I never heard from him or the company again. Maybe I was being paid back for refusing to take a reduced salary on the second Spoleto trip. It felt like a shabby move on Jerry's part.

# * Chapter 14 *

*I* was angry. My place with the well-paying Oldsmobile Show had been taken by someone else, and now I had no job at all. It was spring. The fall shows were several months away, so I was back to the unemployment line.

City Center again came to my rescue. They were doing a revival of *Pal Joey* with Ralph Beaumont doing the choreography and Bob Fosse playing Joey opposite Carol Bruce who would be playing Vera. Eileen Heckart was doing the "Zip" number, which was a takeoff of Gypsy Rose Lee doing a strip tease.

Ralph hired a great group of old gypsies for the chorus. Dancers Lillian and Marilyn D'Honau, Dorothy Dushock, Betty Linton, Pat Turner, Aura Vaino, Eleanor Rogers, and Billy Mahoney were part of the cast. There were a couple of hundred years of experience embodied in that chorus. Ralph did the most successful "bad" choreography I have ever seen. Usually, "bad" choreography looks bad but Ralph managed to give it character and a point of view, and those dancers ran with it. One of the reviews said the real star of the show was that chorus line.

Carol Bruce had been a favorite of mine since I saw her in an old Ritz Brothers movie. She had been playing the role of Vera in summer stock for years and it fit her to a "T." She had the right persona, the right voice, the right age. She was terrific.

Eileen Heckart was not a musical performer. She was doing

her role as a "stretch." In one scene, Fosse, in awe of her, just fed the cues to her and let her run with the scene. Her song, "Zip," was not so good, but she brought the house down every night. She was not fooled. One night I was giving her a ride to Grand Central on the back of my Lambretta motor scooter, and she said her reception was for who she was, not for how well she did the number. I think she was right.

Joey was a role seemingly made for Fosse, and he was very good in it except that he had a gentle personality that worked against him in the role. After the show opened, I overheard two women talking in the elevator of my apartment building. One asked the other if she had seen *Pal Joey*. The second woman said she hadn't and asked what it was about. The first responded that it "was about this gay guy...." I felt the better part of valor was never to mention this to anyone. It was the last role Fosse was to play on Broadway. He did the choreography for his own numbers, and it was here that he began to solidify his style. Previously he had had great success with *Pajama Game*, *Redhead*, *New Girl in Town*, and *Bells Are Ringing*. He also had a huge flop with *The Conquering Hero*. It was such a disaster that he had his name taken off it, so the show opened without credit for direction or choreography. But the numbers he did in *Joey* for himself and a couple of the girls had that high style and precision for which he justly became famous. On a personal level, he went out of his way to compliment me on my work, and I felt that I had an "in" on his next show.

*Pal Joey* opened in late May to great notices and business. The run was extended for several weeks, and immediately there was talk of moving the show to Broadway. For whatever reasons—contracts, time of year, moving expenses—we did not make the move. The manager of the unemployment office saw my face once again. The City Center revived the show the next summer with Fosse, Viveca Lindfors, and Kay Medford. Ethel Martin did the choreography, but the show did not have the same punch that time around.

*Pal Joey* was a turning point for me. Fosse obviously liked me, and one of the dancers told me that I was one of the few dancers that Fosse admired. Word started coming back to me that people had noticed me and thought that I was exceptional. Compliments were nice to hear.

*Ballets: USA* and the Oldsmobile Show were unavailable to me, so I grabbed the first thing that came along, which happened to be the new Noel Coward show, *Sail Away*. I would rather have done *Kean* with Jack Cole, but I didn't make the cut. Jack gave an interesting audition. He started with eight *grand assembles*, front and back, done slowly. If you could do that well, it was assumed that you had a good ballet technique. From there, he went on to specifics. I've always thought that if I ever held auditions, I would follow Cole's example. I would have liked to have worked for Cole, but I never did. I also auditioned for *How to Succeed in Business Without Really Trying*, which Hugh Lambert was doing. I was called back to the finals, but, again, I didn't make the show. Later on, I had a chance to see the file which the producers, Feuer & Martin, kept for that audition. I got an "A" for dancing and a "B" for singing.

*Sail Away* turned out to be a wonderful and glamorous experience. Noel Coward was directing. His codirector and choreographer was Joe Layton, one of the new "hot" talents on Broadway. The stars of the show were Elaine Stritch and Jean Fenn. The supporting cast were names from the past and present like Margalo Gillmore, Carroll McComas, Margaret Mower, Paula Bauersmith, and Alice Pearce, all wonderful personalities. The newcomers were Grover Dale and Patricia Harty. Once while gossiping over beers, someone said that Coward had said that Patricia Harty, who he had seen in *Fiorello* as a replacement for Pat Stanley, would be the next Gertrude Lawrence. Everyone dismissed that idea until Hugh Lambert said, "Maybe Coward was right. Gertrude Lawrence couldn't sing or dance either."

*Sail Away* was about a May-December romance between a younger man, James Hurst, and an older woman, Jean Fenn, aboard a cruise ship with Elaine Stritch as the cruise director providing the comic relief. Jean was from the Metropolitan Opera and sang like a bird. She was also a handsome blonde woman, the type you would find in silver plate ads. Carroll McComas had been a star of the *Princess* musicals in the Teens and Twenties. Margalo Gillmore, whose father was instrumental in the formation of Actor's Equity, had been an ingenue in the Twenties and Thirties. She'd come out of retirement to play Mother Darling in Mary Martin's *Peter Pan.* Alice Pearce was famous as Lucy Schmeeler in *On the Town.* There was history everywhere you looked.

We rehearsed the show in studios on Second Avenue on the Lower East Side, then went to Boston for the tryout. Just before we left for Boston, Carroll McComas was written out of the show, along with one of my favorite songs, "The Bronxville Darby and Jones." She was just too old and couldn't move around the set. The number was restored when the show played London. We did a lot of socializing in Boston. Kennedy was president, and the Summer White House was in Hyannis Port. The combination of Noel Coward and the Kennedy's made for a lot of glitter around Boston that summer. During the opening night performance, the throaty laugh of Judy Garland could be heard in the audience. Unfortunately, her laugh did not influence the reviewers—our reviews were not very good, not awful, but not very good. The re-writes began; the troubles began, and the celebrities arrived.

One actor, James Prichitt, played a sot, and everyday it seemed that one of his lines was cut until he was left with just one line. Inevitably the day arrived when that line was cut, and the cast applauded—it had become a running joke. James remained in the show playing the sot without lines, then went on to great success on television.

However, the problem with the show was not James Prichitt. The problem was the costumes for Jean Fenn. Helene Pons had done the costumes, but except for the uniforms and the

Arab costumes, the rest were mostly bought off the rack. Every night, Jean would turn up in new dresses, but during the daily production meetings, she and her husband decided that Jean's dresses were not right. So, every day, Helene had to go out and buy new dresses. Not surprisingly, the show did not improve.

The show remained chic, however. The Lunts were there, the Crouses were there, and Kay Thompson was there. There were many receptions at which I spent my time trying to recognize famous people. Jacqueline Kennedy came to the show and came backstage afterwards, probably as much for her own publicity as for ours. She didn't have much to say, but she was new to the job and was probably just learning to work a reception line. My favorite First Lady for working the line was that old Army wife, Mamie Eisenhower. When she came down the line, she convinced you that she wanted to be there and was interested in you.

One night after the show, Joe Layton gave a party for the dancers in his room at the Ritz Hotel. In the middle of a game of charades, there was a knock on the door. It was Noel Coward in his dressing gown and slippers looking miffed that he had not been invited to the party. The oversight was quickly rectified, and he joined in the charades. His side lost, and he looked slightly miffed again. He was a wonderful person to work for, always calm, kind, and friendly with his famous "press on" in tandem with Joe's "garbage."

I had driven my motor scooter to Boston, so on days off I was able to explore the Boston area. I went up to Marblehead and out to Concord. Pat Ferrier and I spent an afternoon at Thoreau's Walden Pond in which Pat wanted to soak her sandals. Pat was a wonderful, delightful person with a streak of romanticism. When we moved the show to Philadelphia, I drove my motor scooter twelve hours through the night to New York, put the scooter in the garage, and then caught a bus to Philly.

In Philadelphia, the spit hit the fan. Coward had decided to rewrite the show eliminating Jean Fenn and combining her role with Elaine Stritch's role. It was a great improvement, but some wonderful music for a soprano was lost because there was no way that Elaine could sing "This Is a Changing World," which the great Joan Sutherland later recorded. Rumor had it that Fenn's husband's parting shot at Coward was to call him a fag. When the company heard this, there were lots of chuckles and talk of the pot calling the kettle black.

In Philadelphia, we played the Forrest Theatre. It was quite an odd theater, although pleasant. It was finished before they realized that the architect had forgotten to plan for dressing rooms. To rectify the problem, they built dressing rooms in a building across an alley behind the theater with a tunnel under the alley to connect the dressing rooms and the theater.

Jean Fenn was gone, so while we rehearsed the new version of the show during the day, Annamary Dickey replaced Fenn in the old version of the show that we did at night. Annamary was wonderful. She sang beautifully and played innuendo marvelously. It made me wonder what would have happened to *Sail Away* if she had been cast in the role originally.

During the day, the new show was rehearsed. Bits and pieces that made some sense were inserted into the show we did at night. One day, I was standing in the wings while Stritch and Coward were sitting on stage, obviously going over a scene, although their voices were so low I couldn't hear them. When they finished, Noel passed me on the way out and said, "The lady can act."

Not only could Elaine act, she was also superb at putting over a musical number. "Why Do the Wrong People Travel?" was her eleven o'clock showstopper, which she did solo in front of the curtain. The song was witty, and Elaine did it brilliantly. There was a rumor that Elaine had a "drinking problem," but if she was nipping in the dressing room, I never saw evidence on stage. She did miss a couple of performances in Philadelphia due to laryngitis, which led to an amusing incident one night. Her understudy, Betty Jane Watson, was not really up on the part—who could have been without rehearsals and with the show changing every day? In one scene, she was to ask Mrs. Spencer-Bollard, played by Alice Pearce, if she would like to engage in a game of shuffleboard. Mrs. Spencer-Bollard replied rather haughtily that she would not and Betty Jane was supposed to say, "You're so right, it's silly to chase those little discs around the deck." Betty Jane didn't get the line quite right and instead said, "You're so right, it's silly to chase those little dicks around the deck." During the scene, the dancers were lying around the stage as if they were tanning. We heard the doors at the back of the auditorium open as Coward, Layton, and the bigwigs ran into the street howling with laughter. I'm sure the audience could see our stomachs pumping up and down as we lay there laughing.

Elaine had her own debacle after we had opened in New York. In one scene she would be walking her dog on the deck. She had some business with the dog, and when James Hurst came on stage, a steward would take the dog and Elaine would begin a romantic scene with Hurst. A couple of the company members had their own dogs traveling with them. One night the scene was attempted with two dogs. The number of dogs playing the scene started growing, and by the time we opened, there were six or seven dogs in the scene. Inevitably, one night one of the dogs stopped and did its business on stage, so when the steward came out to take the dogs, he brought some paper towels to clean up the mess. James Hurst's next line was, "We're getting near land. I can smell it in the air." Elaine was the best I had ever seen at handling a "break-up" situation. She didn't hold it in, but rather went with the laugh and released the tension. She gave the line a new ironic meaning, and besides getting some unexpected laughs, it allowed her to get on with the performance.

Philadelphia, being close to New York, got a lot of New York professionals in the audience. Some were invited to give criticism, and others came out of curiosity. Every evening rumors flew around about who was in the audience. Ava

Gardner was there. Katherine Cornell was there. Anybody who was anybody was there, and there were a lot of them. The show was improving, so we thought we had a good chance of being a big hit in New York.

At the same time we were in Philadelphia, *Let It Ride*, a musical version of *Three Men On a Horse* with George Gobel, and *How to Succeed in Business Without Really Trying* were also on tryout. We were invited to those shows. The general consensus was that *Let It Ride* was a hit, but that *How to Succeed* wasn't, and also, that we might be. It turned out in the reverse order. Hugh Lambert had won the job as choreographer of *How to Succeed* on the strength of his work on the Oldsmobile Show the previous year when he had done that one spectacular number. Unfortunately, he seemed to have only one bullet in his gun. The big dance number in *How to Succeed* was the same number he had done for the Oldsmobile Show with different costumes and different music but the same steps and patterns. By the time *How to Succeed* opened in Philadelphia, Bob Fosse had been called in to "doctor" the show. When it opened in New York, the choreography was credited to Hugh Lambert, but the "musical staging" was credited to Fosse. Hugh's work was the forgettable part of the show.

We moved to the Broadhurst Theatre on West Forty-Fourth Street. *Sail Away* was supposed to take place on the *Caronia*, and we took publicity photos on the ship. Our opening night party was also supposed to be on the *Caronia*, but then our opening night was changed, so the opening night party was also changed to the *Queen Mary*. Sadly, because of that ship's turnaround time, the party was changed to the more prosaic Sardi's East.

The opening was like a Broadway opening in the movies. I invited Mom to come to New York for it. From the stage, one could look out and see all those famous faces sitting in the audience, at least in the first couple of rows. Backstage, stories were swapped about who had spotted whom in the audience. So that her laugh wouldn't steal the show, Judy Garland was not allowed to attend. A double decker bus had been hired to transport us across town to the party after the show. When I met Mom at the stage door, guess who we saw sitting in the front seat of the upper deck? Margaret Truman. I'm sure Mom enjoyed telling that story to her friends back in Flint.

The walls of Sardi's East were decorated with autographed caricatures of Noel Coward. They didn't last long on the walls. I got one for Mom. Mr. Coward was Mr. Gracious as he came around to all the tables, met Mom, shook her hand, and kissed her on the cheek. Mom was not one to obviously swell up with pride, but I think she lived off this night for a long time. Sardi's was packed with the famous and the talented. Myrna Loy, Thurber, the Crouses, and Marlene Dietrich. For a time, Margalo Gillmore took Mom under her wing, introduced her to the famous, and undoubtedly told her what a great son she had raised. As we were leaving, I pointed to the bar and said, "There's Lauren Bacall."

Mom stared a moment and said, "That doesn't look right."

I then said, "That's Jason Robards, Jr. next to her."

Mom stared again and replied, "That looks better."

For an opening night present, Joe Layton and Noel recorded "The Bronxville Darby and Jones" and "This Is a Changing World" in campy versions. Noel presented each of the cast members with autographed copies of his play *Waiting in The Wings*. Jere Admire received the gypsy robe. By this time, the original gypsy robe had been retired, and I think the life preserver that *Sail Away* attached to the new robe was its first memento.

Unfortunately, the reviews were middling. We limped along until February then were forced to close because we just weren't selling enough tickets. *Sail Away* was a happy experience. It had some of my favorite music; it was a happy company, and during the run I acquired my new companion for the next thirteen years, a mongrel dog, part Basenji, from Bide-A-Wee. I named her Ari after Aristotle Onassis.

I left the show a week before closing in order to have a week off before starting a new show. I left Ari with a friend and went to Bermuda, hoping for some sun, but it rained most of the week.

# * Chapter 15 *

My next show was *Bravo Giovanni*, another May-September romance set against a battle between the owner of a small mom-and-pop restaurant and a chain restaurant. The owner of the small restaurant builds a tunnel into the chain's kitchen and siphons off the food. It had music and lyrics by Milton Schafer and Ronny Graham, both of whom I still think are exceptional. The star of the show was Cesare Siepi from the Metropolitan Opera. His love interest was Michelle Lee who was then still in her teens. It was her second Broadway show, the first being a small revue that didn't last long. Carol Haney was doing the dances. Maria Karnilova and her husband, George S. Irving, were playing character parts. George had been in *Shinbone Alley*, and Maria had been in *Ballets: USA*. Most of the dancers were the same ones who did the Oldsmobile Show. One tends to keep working with the same people.

We rehearsed *Bravo* in Room 302 of the Variety Arts Studio on West Forty-Sixth Street. Variety Arts is now a parking lot due to a fire of suspicious origins a few years ago. It was run by my old friend Fergus Hunter. The front door was guarded by the switchboard operator, Edie Kramer, who is fondly remembered as "Broadway Rose." Besides being the place where a good proportion of shows rehearsed, the studios were rented out for auditions, vocalizing, and classes. It was also a spot for socializing and gossip. A few minutes spent at Variety Arts allowed one to be up on the current gossip about what was happening or about to happen. Edie knew everything, or, if she didn't know, she could make educated guesses. All calls, incoming and outgoing, went through Edie, and over the years she pretty well knew which phone number belonged to whom and the callers' voices. She didn't actually listen in on conversations, but she could add things up. If a producer was talking to an agent who was looking for a show for his or her client, you could pretty well bet that there was a cast change coming. Edie was amazing. She could hold two conversations at one time and still remember three numbers that she was supposed to dial while connecting callers through the old-fashioned switchboard comprised of cables and trunk lines. If you were looking for someone and they were not at Variety Arts, Edie probably knew where they were or when they might be there.

Upstairs there were three floors of studios. Room 302 was the favorite of most choreographers and producers. The room was large and had more depth than the other studios, even though the depth was cut by posts going across the room. There was frequently a show being rehearsed in that room, and if not, it was probably reserved for a show about to start rehearsals. Carol Haney always used Room 302, and Fosse had a key to the studio so that he could come in at night to do his pre-production work. If you walked down West Forty-Sixth Street at eleven or twelve o'clock at night, looked up and saw lights burning on the third floor, it was a good probability that Fosse was working on something. The Oldsmobile Shows always rehearsed in Room 302, but this was the first time I had rehearsed there. Productions usually rented a small room as a temporary office, a large room for musical numbers, and another room for the book rehearsals.

Carol's way of working was to come in the morning and already have a couple of dance combinations planned. Once those were learned, she relaxed, told a few jokes, kidded around for a while, disappeared for a few minutes, and then came back with more combinations. Luther was indispensable to her. On the first day of rehearsals, Carol, with Luther leading the way, started on the "big" dance number that featured Maria Karnilova. By mid-afternoon, during a break, I was sitting next to Maria who complained that her feet hurt because of the heels she was wearing. I suggested that she do the rehearsals in flats, and she said, "No, if I'm going to dance in heels, I have to rehearse in them." The next day she appeared in flats, which I remarked upon, and she said, "If I can do it in flats, I can do it in heels." Attitudes change, particularly when the feet hurt.

The set for the number was a little strange because there was more room on stage left than on stage right. While staging the number, Carol put Maria and a couple of guys on either side of her in the center and all the other dancers on stage left, except me. I felt rather lonely over on stage right all by myself. Carol's assistant pointed this out to Carol who said, "Gene can hold it." I lived on that compliment for weeks.

Carol did a "kitchen ballet" for this show that was brilliant, possibly the best thing she ever did. It wasn't a dance number as much as a pantomime, a Mack Sennet romp with pizza makers, salad makers, and an assembly line of cooks and waiters running around the stage with food and utensils flying through the air.

For me it was a pleasant time. I loved working for Carol, and I liked the show. I also had continuous employment for most of the year. We went to Detroit's Fisher Theatre for the tryout. The newly restored Fisher Theatre in the Fisher Tower was the new place for tryouts. They had a good subscription series which pretty much guaranteed that a show would break even in Detroit. It was far enough away from New York that the naysayers wouldn't be in the audience. Only the *Variety* review and the local papers' reviews would get back to New York. It was also very convenient for me because Flint was only sixty miles from Detroit. Mom treated my brother Jim and his family to a trip to see the show. When the cast album came out, I sent one to my sister-in-law, and I think she wore the record out.

After Detroit, we moved to the Forrest Theatre in Philadelphia for a couple of weeks before going to New York. I was beginning to like playing Philly. I had made friends there, so I always had a lot of parties to go to in my free time. Then we moved on to New York and the Broadhurst Theatre. We got middling to good reviews, though they weren't good enough to drive an audience to the theater. However, we did have a quarter of a million dollars in advance sales to theater parties that allowed us to run and perhaps build an audience by word of mouth. Hope springs eternal. Unfortunately, the advance sale was mostly for the fall, and it was only May. So, by early June, it was obvious that audiences were not going to build, at least for the summer. It was decided we would take a break for the summer. Negotiations with various unions were conducted, and permission was granted to close the show for six to eight weeks during the summer and reopen in the fall. The producers would have liked a longer break, but that was all the unions would agree to. The cast members would not be held to their contracts.

We closed for the summer, but it was too late to do the Oldsmobile Show that year, so I had a couple of months to spend at the beach. The big problem started when I was called by the producers to come to the office and sign my contract to reopen *Bravo Giovanni*. That same day, Bob Fosse was having the first auditions for a new show he was doing called *Little Me*. I had a big problem between desire and loyalty. Carol had been so good to me giving me lots of work, and I felt I owed her the loyalty. At the same time, I wanted to work for Fosse. But, these were the first auditions—the finals wouldn't be until the following week. What to do?

I went to the audition and managed to speak to Fosse. I explained my predicament to him, that I was supposed to sign a contract that afternoon and asked him if it was possible, that if I auditioned, would he be able to give me an answer that same day. He was understanding, but said he wouldn't be able to make any decisions that day. So, shrouded in loyalty and the idea that a "bird in the hand…," I went and signed my contract for the reopening of *Bravo Giovanni*.

That evening, Gwen Verdon, Fosse's wife, called me and said Bob wanted me for *Little Me*. The last time I had auditioned for him, he called me personally to tell me I didn't make the show. This time he had his wife, a Broadway star, call me. Is it any wonder that dancers adored Fosse? Unfortunately, I had to tell her that I had signed a contract for *Bravo*.

We rehearsed *Bravo* for a week, then reopened. It was too early. That big advance was for October, and we were doing no business. The losses for September would have been too great to sustain, so we closed after a week or two. Shows never seem to be able to pick up any momentum after a hiatus.

I was a little depressed because not much seemed to be happening. One night, however, I received a call from Phil Friedman, the stage manager of *Little Me*, which was on tryout in Philadelphia. Fosse was looking for a swing dancer for the show. Merritt Thompson, Fosse's assistant, told me that when Fosse and he were discussing who to get as a swing, they were going through a list of possible dancers. My name came up because *Bravo* had closed. When my name was mentioned, Fosse said, "Get him." I didn't hesitate in accepting, and it was decided that I should wait for the company to come back to New York the following week rather than going to Philadelphia immediately. That telephone call was the beginning of a long association with Fosse, Thompson, Friedman, and the producers Feuer & Martin.

# * Chapter 16 *

*L*ittle Me is my all-time favorite show. It was based upon Patrick Dennis's satiric novel about the rise of a film star from the backwoods to Hollywood dowager who leaves a swath of dead lovers in her path. The adaptation of the book was done by Neil Simon with lyrics and music by Carolyn Leigh and Cy Coleman. It was produced by Feuer & Martin who had a great track record including *Where's Charley, Guys and Dolls,* and the current big hit on Broadway, *How to Succeed in Business Without Really Trying. Little Me* was directed by Feuer. Fosse did the choreography.

Sid Caesar, making his return to Broadway after more than a decade in television, was the star of the show, playing multiple roles of the lovers of the leading lady, Belle. In one scene he played two at the same time. Belle, was played by Virginia Martin as the young Belle and Nancy Andrews as the older Belle. I understand that Kitty Carlisle had been intended as the older woman but dropped out after the death of her husband, Moss Hart. Swen Swenson was the leading dancer. Mort Marshall and Joey Faye, two old vaudevillians, played minor parts. I love old vaudevillians—they are irrepressible. One day, I was in Joey and Mort's dressing room while Seymour Kravitz, the press agent for the show, was also there. Seymour said that there was a dichotomy in regard to something or other. Mort immediately turned to Joey and said, "Joey, use dichotomy in a sentence."

Without batting an eyelash, Joey said, "Kay (a well-known female singer) said that Gloria (a well-known female agent) made a dichotomy." They were quick and had probably waited years to pull off that line.

The following Monday morning, after the call from Philadelphia, I went down to the Lunt-Fontanne Theatre on West Forty-Sixth Street where the show was to open. I read for the production stage manager, Phil Friedman, and then signed a contract as swing dancer and assistant stage manager, which paid an extra ten dollars a week. Phil then sent me next door to Variety Arts, Room 302, to join the dancers' rehearsal.

Fosse greeted me when I walked into the rehearsal. He gave me a quick introduction to the other dancers, some of whom I knew but most of whom I didn't. He then asked the dancers to run through a number and jokingly said to be good because I was after their jobs. I sat beside Fosse and his assistant, Merritt Thompson, while the dancers did a run through of "The Rich Kids Rag." I was absolutely stunned. It was brilliant, but it seemed so complicated with everyone doing something so stylized and different at the same time. I wondered if I could ever learn all the different parts and how they fit together. Suddenly, I was full of apprehension about my adequacy, but at this point nobody was worrying about me. I was told to pick up what I could, then put into a scene in order to relieve someone else of a quick change, and then I was pretty much ignored. Later during a run through at the theater, I was given a flashlight and told to follow Virginia Martin around and provide light for her while she made her costume changes in the wings.

*Little Me* was a lightning fast show with a small cast that doubled in many small roles. There were few singers or dancers who didn't have some small role, and many had several parts to fill. After any dance or musical number, the wings were filled with people doing quick changes and avoiding the moving sets in order to dash back on stage for a line or some business. Some nights I wondered if the show backstage wasn't equally as interesting as the one on stage.

When I first started to do musicals, a normal cast consisted of eight male and eight female dancers. Dancers learned the lyrics to the songs and either sang along or mouthed the lyrics if they couldn't hit the high notes. As the pay scale for Equity performers went up, the size of the casts went down. First, the number of singers was decreased, and the dancers were expected to pick up the slack. Then the singers were expected to dance a little. If you could sing and dance fairly well, you were in. Of course, it's easier to sing passably than it is to dance passably, so pure singers began to be cut out of the business, and the sound changed from head voices to chest voices. Singers, in order to get a job, needed to be able to handle small character roles, a position that dancers didn't usually fill because they were younger. Some singers made careers of being able to sing an especially high or low note as well as being able to do a character part.

Fosse was the real star of *Little Me*. It was the show where his style—splaying fingers, thrusting hips, isolating body parts—really and definitively took root. He created quite an atmosphere. I understood that when he started choreography, he was as much of an ogre as Jerome Robbins, but somehow he learned the old adage about honey catching more flies than vinegar. Fosse's dancers and singers loved him, and I think he loved them. He played on that love. A Fosse dancer would have rather broken a leg than disappoint him. In the years that I was associated with Fosse, I never heard a cast member speak ill of him. All the dancers loved and respected Fosse. We felt honored and special to be able to work for him. The dark side of Fosse, the drugs and womanizing, that later were written about and became the subject of his autobiographical film, *All That Jazz*, was not yet evident. Maybe I was just naive or not observant. I think he was on pills, but that was just to keep going through the long hours of rehearsals plus the late hours spent preparing for the next day. All in all, working for Fosse was a joyous experience.

When Fosse was doing a show, Gwen Verdon, his wife, was the unofficial assistant choreographer. Gwen was a big Broadway musical comedy star in her own right, but she was also very down to earth and very protective of Fosse. If Gwen gave a correction during a rehearsal, who was going to dispute it? Besides, she was probably right. If she wasn't at rehearsals, she'd check with Edie at the switchboard to see if rehearsals had broken so that she could have dinner waiting when Bob got home. I never worked a show with Gwen as the star, but friends who had worked with her claimed that she had eyes in the back of her head. She could exit the stage from a big number and ask why some dancer behind her had goofed a step or had a hand or arm out of position.

During the Philadelphia tryout of *Little Me*, there was one number for the female dancers that wasn't working. Fosse rewrote one of the show's musicals numbers, "Real Live Girl" and created a new number for the male dancers. The night that the new version went into the show to a great reception from the audience, Fosse went into the lobby of the Erlanger Theatre and did an ecstatic back flip. Another time, Carolyn Leigh, the lyricist, was upset about something being changed in the show. She went out and found a traffic cop, dragged him into the lobby of the theater, and demanded that the poor man stop the show.

After returning to New York, the company rehearsed for a couple of days while the set was being hung and gave a couple of previews. Finally, *Little Me* opened. By word of mouth, it was supposed to be the hit of the season. It wasn't. We had gotten reviews that should have made it one of the big ones, but it didn't work out that way. At first we had sold out houses, and Swen Swenson was the talk of the town for his modified striptease to the tune of "I've Got Your Number." But word of mouth started working against us. Sid Caesar was coughing his way through performances. He was mumbling. One night as soon as Sid made his entrance, the dreaded "louder" came sailing from out of the back of the auditorium. Sid was brilliant when the audience liked him, but if they didn't love him immediately, he seemed to back off his performance. A few months later, *Oliver* opened and became the big hit of the season.

As soon as the show opened, I spent the next couple of weeks in a rehearsal studio at Variety Arts with Merritt Thompson learning everyone's parts in all the numbers. Merritt was Feuer & Martin's regular dance captain. It was his job to keep the numbers in top shape. Sometimes he was doing it for two or three shows at the same time. During *Little Me* he also worked *How to Succeed* across the street at the Forty-Sixth Street Theatre. Usually, unless there was an accident like a sprained ankle, the swing dancer didn't have to worry about going on until several weeks after opening when a little boredom would begin to set in among the dancers and they would start calling in sick. There had also been a change in union rules. Previously, if you missed a performance you were docked an eighth of a week's pay, but women had campaigned for a day off a month, and that perk could not be given just to women, so Equity won all ensemble members a day off per month with pay. It was amazing how many cast members were not of "the show must go on" tradition and started getting sick after that provision was added to the Equity contract. As soon as word went out that I knew the show, I expected that I would be called upon rather quickly. I even took bets with a friend as to who would be the first to take a night off. I won.

So, for the rest of the run, as soon as the half hour check-in had passed and we knew that someone would be out of that performance, Merritt and I met to go over all that person's numbers, bits of stage business, small scenes, and which of my stage-managing duties would have to be covered by someone else. Merritt was a wonderful throwback to the idea that the performance is the most important thing in the world. After conferring with Merritt, I dressed for the performance and took my script and placed it strategically in the wings so that I could refer to it as the show progressed. I was having a ball and eventually covered for the entire ensemble. One night during a flu epidemic, there were three or four people missing from the cast, and I found myself meeting myself as I made an exit and had to go right back on for the next scene. At the end of a small scene with Sid, as I exited, Sid gave me a pat on the back. I wasn't even certain up to that point if Sid knew there was chaos around him. He was neither friendly nor unfriendly with the cast, so his acknowledgement of me was nice. I think it was this night when Nancy Cushman, a character actress in the show, delivered one of my favorite lines. She looked at me and said, "My, you're as busy as a bird dog in a high wind."

I made some lifelong friends in *Little Me*. Merritt became my buddy. Phil Friedman, the production stage manager, became my social friend and bridge partner. Virginia Martin, the leading lady and backbone of the show, also became my buddy. Virginia was from Tennessee and possessed a Mermanesque voice—not pretty, but loud. There was no need to put a microphone on Virginia because she could project to the back of the house. The previous year she had had a huge success playing the sexpot Hedy LaRue in *How to Succeed*. She didn't have a large bosom, but she had cleavage, and when she wore a thirty-eight bra, it looked natural. No matter what happened on stage, no matter how many lines were goofed or what business was added extemporaneously, Virginia was never thrown off balance.

On opening night, I remember seeing Lucille Ball backstage. I heard her say that she'd better go up and see John Sharpe who had been in her show, *Wildcat*, the previous season. The biggest star of television climbed four floors to a chorus boy's dressing room to congratulate him on his performance. Some of the big ones are really down to earth.

After *Little Me* opened, I started taking acting classes. I had studied briefly with Earle Hyman at Uta Hagen's school in the Village. Now I started studying with Eve Collyer. Eve held one class for working actors at Variety Arts starting at eleven o'clock at night. Ferg had given her a key to the studio, so after the curtains came down, a group of us gathered at Variety Arts. It was a great time for classes. After a show, the energy is up, and it was nicer to use it in an acting class than drinking in a bar. Eve's classes were exciting, and sometimes it was after four o'clock in the morning before we left the studio. Some of the other students were Christopher Walken, Virginia Vestoff, and Laurence Guittard.

*Little Me* stumbled on until June when diminishing audiences forced the closing. It was a big disappointment to me because I really loved the show. It was fun to be doing the Fosse numbers, and I enjoyed the challenge of swinging the show, all except for one spot. Fosse had staged a great entrance for Sid Caesar. At the beginning of the show, Sid was a teenager. A group on stage looked off stage and said, "Here he comes now," referring to Sid's character. Whereupon a chorus dancer, dressed in Sid's costume, did back flips across the stage from right and exiting left. Sid then entered from left, saying, "I guess I over flipped." Unfortunately, I couldn't do back flips. We substituted cartwheels, but even then, I was in danger of going into the orchestra pit. I was afraid I ruined his entrances the nights I had to do that part.

When the show closed, it was just in time to pick up the Oldsmobile Show for that year. Later on when I was in San Francisco and almost at the end of the Oldsmobile tour, Phil Friedman, who was back on *How to Succeed*, called and said that someone was leaving the show and that they would hold the position for me until I got back to New York. I readily accepted because *How to Succeed* was still one of the big hit shows in New York. It had opened the previous year, and it was the show that President Kennedy had chosen to see on one of his New York visits. Just inside the stage door hung a picture of Kennedy and his group taking their seats.

As soon as I returned to New York, Merritt rehearsed me for *How to Succeed*, and I went into the show a week later. This was comfortable. I now had a job that was certain to last a couple of years at least. Since *West Side Story*, I had not been in a show that was guaranteed to run more than six months. And, of course, I was working for Fosse, so I was happy.

One thing in *How to Succeed* that I hated to do was jump into the orchestra pit. Fosse liked to break the fourth wall, and in the "Coffee Break" number, my character, frustrated at not having any coffee, had to take the plunge. As I moved to the front of the stage apron, a violinist in the orchestra pit moved her chair and herself under the overhang. There was a white circle painted on the floor for me to aim for, but as I jumped, I always saw the bow of the violinist sticking out, and I was petrified that I would impale myself on the bow or hit the back of my head on the apron. Probably the only night I did it comfortably was after dinner with one of the stage managers. We had shared a meal between the afternoon and evening performance. He was the type who refilled your glass before you finished your drink so you never had any idea of how much you'd consumed. That night I was feeling no pain from I don't know how many martinis. I landed in a heap after the jump, but I was so relaxed that I didn't hurt myself. I'd hate to do that stunt in a touring show where the pit changed every week.

One November morning, I got out of bed to hear the radio announcing the assassination of President Kennedy. I took my dog to the curb, then like the rest of the world, I was glued all day to the television. It wasn't long before the telephone rang, and one of the stage managers of *How to Succeed* told me that the performance was cancelled that night. I was a little surprised, but then I had no idea how one was supposed to react to an assassination. Soon the television began announcing that businesses were closing. The city became very quiet. That night I called a friend, and we decided we'd had enough of our apartments, so we went out. I picked him up on my motor scooter, and we drove through a darkened Times Square. The streets were empty. Everything was closed, even the bars. Eventually we found a bar that was open with a few patrons, but after one drink we decided we might as well go home because there was no socializing going on. We might as well sit in front of the television like everyone else. Two performances were cancelled, then the arguments began. Equity deemed that the assassination was "an act of God," and therefore, the producers did not have to pay us for the cancelled performances. Our bereavement was going to cost us.

Another night, former Vice President Nixon made a backstage visit with Mrs. Nixon and their daughters, Tricia and Julie, who evidently had a crush on Robert Morse and was the reason for the visit. Nixon was absolutely charming and funny, not at all like the dour man in the news. Mrs. Nixon stood at the back of the stage staring out at the house, obviously not wanting to take part and patiently waiting for it to be over. Most of the cast had come back on stage to meet Mr. Nixon, although there were a couple who expressed their disapproval of him by not coming on stage.

Liza Minnelli was going out with one of the dancers in *How to Succeed*. She was a sweet, polite, and quiet kid. Every night when we finished the show and started for the dressing rooms, Liza would be sitting on the steps waiting for her boyfriend. One afternoon, she walked into the dressing room expecting to find her friend and caught me in the "all together." She apologized and backed out. When I left the dressing room, she was sitting on the steps and again said, "I'm so sorry." Later, in my insecurity, I wondered if the apology was for walking in or for what she saw.

We began to hear rumors that *Little Me* was going to be sent on tour, making a few stops along the way to the West Coast, then be part of the Los Angeles/San Francisco Light

Opera season. The Light Opera was established and run by Edwin Lester. Usually they presented four shows a season, each playing both Los Angeles and San Francisco, and sometimes Pasadena. They had a large subscription base and usually imported a show from Broadway, did a couple of revivals, and frequently an original show, which was always announced as a "pre-Broadway" production but usually did not go beyond the Light Opera season. A couple of shows in its history, however, did make it to Broadway, such as *Song of Norway* and *Kismet*. I was asked to assist Fosse at the auditions.

During the auditions, I pushed hard for a dancer named Kathryn Doby, a Hungarian refugee. She became one of my dear friends and later became Fosse's assistant on *Pippin*, *Chicago*, and the movie versions of *Sweet Charity* and *Cabaret*. She is also a sensational bridge player. At the end of the audition, Phil Friedman asked me how much I wanted to be paid to assist Fosse on staging the show as well as to tour as dance captain and swing dancer. I knew from the rapidity of their acceptance that I had not asked for enough, but I was happy because I loved *Little Me*, and it was an honor to work with Bob Fosse.

Just before we started rehearsals, I dropped into Variety Arts. Edie told me that Carol Haney was in Room 302. I went upstairs, knocked on the door, and entered. Carol and Luther Henderson were there. Carol said that she was starting *Funny Girl* the next day, and that she had absolutely nothing prepared. After a little socializing and some "good lucks," I left to let her get on with her work. It was the last time I saw Carol.

# * Chapter 17 *

---

S id Caesar, Virginia Martin, Nancy Andrews, and
Swen Swenson had agreed to tour with *Little Me*. This
made it possible to advertise it as the original cast.
Most Broadway stars did not take their shows on the road, so
the road companies were populated with lesser names. This
sometimes created resentment in the cities they played, especially in Chicago and with the main critic there, Claudia Cassidy. Fortunately, we weren't scheduled to play Chicago. After
a month's rehearsal in New York, we went to Rochester for a
week, mostly for technical rehearsals and to play for a weekend.
Then we went on to Toronto where there was a lot of excitement, though not caused by us. We had good reviews and full
houses, but we were overshadowed by Richard Burton and
Elizabeth Taylor. Burton was rehearsing his revival of *Hamlet*
in the same Toronto theater we were in. He was in the midst of
his "scandalous" romance with Taylor. The press and the pho-
tographers were always outside the stage door. Whenever I saw
Taylor, I was amazed at her beauty. She really was spectacular.

Mom and some of her cousins made the trip to Toronto to
see the show. I introduced her to Virginia who was so taken
with her that in one scene she worked in an ad lib, calling out
to "Mrs. Tuttle" from the stage.

When dance numbers are rehearsed, usually the tempo

seems impossibly fast. But as you get used to the steps and combinations, the tempo begins to feel comfortable. Then the tempo is increased until it's where the choreographer wants it to be. Then after a while when you're comfortable again, the tempo starts to feel too slow, and you wonder why you ever thought it was too fast. Another phenomenon happens during performance. There are nights when the company collectively complains that the conductor must be trying to catch an early train, and there are other nights when everyone thinks that the conductor is playing a dirge. Not so sure of myself regarding the tempo, when the road company of *Little Me* was set, I timed the numbers with a stop watch so that I knew what they should be. One night, I happened to be timing the show, and during "The Rich Kids Rag," thought it was terribly slow. When the company came off stage, they were all complaining of the dirge-like tempo. I looked at my watch, and the tempo had been exactly as set. Later, I timed Swen Swenson doing "I've Got Your Number," and again it seemed slow to me. When Swen came off stage cursing the slow tempo, I looked at my watch—and a four-minute number had been three seconds faster than was set. Who knows why it feels different from time to time—maybe it's atmospheric pressure.

We moved on to Cleveland for two weeks before going to Pittsburgh. There had been rumors that the Pittsburgh booking was not solid. In Cleveland, we heard that Pittsburgh was cancelled, and we were going to Chicago instead. Evidently the producers had known that getting the show into the Nixon Theatre in Pittsburgh was a tight fit, as some of the set would have to be stored in an alley. They finally decided it was not feasible and quickly booked the show into the Blackstone Theatre in Chicago, which had a couple of weeks available. The Blackstone didn't have the seating capacity we needed, but the stage was big enough to hold all the sets. It was a fortuitous decision.

We were a smash hit in Chicago. Even Claudia Cassidy, the

Chicago critic who usually panned the New York shows, raved. We immediately sold out for the entire engagement. Love poured across the footlights towards Sid Caesar, and he responded with his best performances. *Little Me* probably belonged in a small, intimate house, but the economics of theater did not allow that. Our two-week stopgap booking could probably have been a six-month run in Chicago.

One night near the end of the two weeks, I was paged for a phone call at the stage door. It was my brother, Jim, telling me that Mom had been in an accident. She had left Jim's house one Sunday afternoon and, driving at thirty miles per hour, had blacked out, gone off the road, hit a tree, and totaled the car. Fortunately, she had gone off the right side of the road and not into oncoming traffic. She broke an arm and was a mass of bruises. Jim fainted when he saw her. The blackout was never explained, but it was the beginning of several of them. She always claimed that she had sustained some brain damage from hitting her head. After the accident, she had some minor problems with memory, but maybe it was just senility setting in—it happens to all of us. We were scheduled to be in Detroit the next week, so I told Jim that I would come up to Flint on my way. When I saw Virginia that night, she asked me if the call had been bad news. Somehow she sensed it.

We moved on to Detroit for a month, and for the first couple of weeks until Mom was released from the hospital, I got up early on non-matinee days to take the bus to Flint to visit her for a couple of hours. Then I would return to Detroit in time for the show. Near the end of the engagement, Jim brought his family to see the show and have dinner. Mom was proud as a peacock that Jim's twins, her grandsons, ordered frog legs and were not fazed by the finger bowls.

From Detroit, we flew to San Francisco. The sets went by jet, but the cast took a prop plane and had a rough flight. A good many of the airsick bags were used. My dog had flown with the sets and was calmly waiting for me at the airport. When

I first bought a wooden pet carrier from American Airlines, I put it in the living room with the door open and her toys inside hoping that she would get used to the carrier. She wouldn't go near it. However, as soon as we got to the airport for check-in, she jumped right in without a fuss. I guess she sensed that it was either get in or stay behind.

In San Francisco, we played the Curran Theatre, one of my favorite theaters in the country. It has a nice capacity and an intimate feel, and is a wonderful theater to play. Some of the Bette Davis film *All About Eve* was filmed there.

Virginia had the use of a courtesy Oldsmobile and had rented a houseboat in Sausalito. The houseboat was nice, but it was moored on some mud flats near the Sausalito airport, and the view wasn't terribly appetizing. Her hairdresser, John, had rented another one on the next dock. One Sunday, Virginia and I decided to take her dresser, Mary, and the men's dresser, a Filipino named Sonny, on a trip to the Big Sur country. Virginia drove with Mary in the front seat and Sonny and my dog and I in the backseat. It was one of those perfect California days until dinner when we stopped at a restaurant south of San Francisco. The restaurant was cantilevered over the ocean, and most of us ordered ribs for dinner. Halfway through dinner, I took a bite of a rib and heard a loud crack in my head. I immediately knew that one of my caps had broken. I stuck my finger in my mouth, found the broken cap, and managed to stick it back on my front tooth. Needless to say, my dinner was finished, and I spent a lot of time exploring my mouth with my tongue to see if the cap was still on the tooth. After dinner and back in the car, we were driving north when we came to Gilroy, Garlic Capital of the World.

I saw it just in time to grab the dog. Two artichoke pickers playing chicken entered the highway from the left without lights. We smashed into them, driving them into a billboard on the right side of the road and us into the southbound lane. I was the only one not knocked unconscious. The first thing I did was feel my tooth with my tongue to see if the cap was still on. I shoved the driver's seat forward. The dog and I got out of the car just in time to hear the screech of brakes and to see a southbound car miss us by inches. Virginia slowly revived. Sonny, in the backseat, was staring straight ahead, saying nothing. Mary, in the front passenger seat, started moaning eerily, and I knew that she was dying. A small crowd started to form, including a priest, which I found foreboding. The artichoke pickers wanted to know if the accident could be settled privately because they had no insurance. Eventually an ambulance arrived and took us to a hospital with Mary still making that dreadful sound. At the hospital, we discovered that Virginia had a big bump on her head and a mean case of whiplash. Sonny was OK, and I suffered only a couple of lacerations across my shins. Mary had broken an ankle, but was not dying despite her moaning. We called a cab to take us back to San Francisco. We had to leave Mary in the hospital. We hoped that because Virginia's driver's license was in her married name, we could keep the whole thing out of the newspapers. Herb Caen, the famous San Francisco gossip columnist, loved stuff like this.

Once in San Francisco, Sonny departed for his hotel. We assumed he was not hurt, but we didn't know for sure. He wasn't talking. We awakened an assistant stage manager to tell him what had happened and to alert the company that Virginia might not be able to perform the next night. We rented a car for Virginia to drive back to Sausalito. I asked Virginia if she was okay. She said she was and took off across the Golden Gate Bridge. I went to my hotel, checking my tooth all the way and wondering how I could find a dentist the next morning.

No sooner than I had gotten to bed, the telephone rang. It was Virginia. She'd gotten back to Sausalito, but she sounded hysterical. I told her I would be right out. I got dressed and found a cab that would take me to Sausalito. When I got there, I knocked on the door, but she wouldn't open it. I could hear her inside, sometimes crying and sometimes ranting, so I kept knocking. Eventually she heard me and opened the door. I poured her a stiff drink and got her to drink it. I suspected it wasn't the first drink she'd had since she'd gotten back to the houseboat, but I couldn't get her to go back to bed because she said she couldn't sleep. I called a hospital, explained the situation, and asked if they could send me a sleeping pill. It amazed me that they sent a messenger with one sleeping pill, which, after some effort, I managed to get Virginia to swallow. As soon as she swallowed the pill, I had the thought that maybe she had already taken some pills and I may have just forced a fatal overdose down her gullet.

I needed a pill myself because I couldn't sleep. I decided to bother Virginia's hairdresser, John, next door. I went out the front door and was halfway to John's boat when I heard the door to Virginia's houseboat slam shut. By the sound, I knew that it was locked. I fruitlessly knocked on John's door. He wasn't home, so I was stuck on the mud flats in the middle of the night.

I took stock of the situation while my tongue was checking out the situation with my cap every couple of minutes. A side door that led to a veranda was ajar, and there was a small rowboat sitting in the water a few yards offshore. After finding a large stick, I started making waves in San Francisco Bay. My plan worked, and eventually the rowboat floated towards me within grabbing distance. I paddled the rowboat with my hands and managed to get to the veranda and back into the houseboat where I immediately unlocked the front door.

Virginia was sleeping. I was getting angry at John for not being home. After a while, figuring that the bars had closed and John must have arrived, I started for his place once again, and, once again, I was half way there when I heard Virginia's door slam again. John still wasn't home. When I returned to Virginia's boat, the door I'd left unlocked was now locked. Finding another stick, I started making waves again. The rowboat was sitting somewhere in the vicinity of where I'd left it. A second miracle, and I was paddling towards the veranda again. When I got back to her houseboat the second time, there was Virginia standing at the door. She had gotten up, found the front door open, and shut and locked it. I got her back into bed.

In the morning, the stage manager came out and took over. He made a doctor's appointment for Virginia, and I took a cab back to San Francisco to find a dentist to give me a temporary cap. That night Virginia went on. She missed a few high notes, but she never missed a performance. She lived by "the show must go on" tradition.

We moved on to Los Angeles where we played an auditorium that presented a few problems. It was actually in a Baptist Church so the censors went through the show and demanded certain changes. We lucked out, and not much had to be changed. A few lines were modified— "You're God damned right, the truth" became "You're gosh darned right, the truth." Our big worry, Swen Swenson's campy "striptease" number, escaped unscathed. It was pretty erotic, but maybe eroticism is in the eye of the beholder. Anyway, nothing in that number had to be changed.

After six weeks in Los Angeles, we moved to Pasadena for a final week, and then the tour was over. We took the train back to New York leaving some of the company in Los Angeles. I think that most shows that go to the West Coast for the Light Opera Season leave some of their cast members behind in L.A. It was, after all, a good way to move. Your transportation was paid, and you had a job for six or seven weeks while you got settled, talked to agents, and prepared to start a career in television or the movies. Most of the company stayed at the Montecito Hotel where the pool was a beehive of gossips and contacts. One never knew who would appear at the pool of the Montecito - visiting actors from New York or Hollywood, luminaries, and visiting friends.

# ✳ *Chapter 18* ✳

B ack in New York, my old friend Phil Friedman hired me to do a new part in *How to Succeed*, so I did six more months in that show. I think that's when I met the delightful Donna McKechnie, who went on to great stardom in *A Chorus Line*. As it always did, business began to wind down, and the show was going to be sent out on tour. Fosse was doing a new show called *Pleasures and Palaces*. We all wanted to be in it. As the auditions approached, we spent a lot of time looking out the dressing room window at Variety Arts across the street. Usually Fosse would be in Room 302 working on the new show. We couldn't see more than an occasional walk or turn, not enough to give us much sense of what he was doing. I understood that if we could have heard it, we would have heard him working to classical music, which he reportedly used to devise the steps and style.

Auditions were held, and several of the dancers from *How to Succeed* were hired, including me and my friend Kathryn Doby, who was then working with the June Taylor Dancers on *The Jackie Gleason Show* down in Miami. It was nice working with her again.

*Pleasures and Palaces* was based on a flop show called *Once There Was a Russian* by Sam and Bella Spewack. Mr. Spewack did the book; Frank Loesser did the music and lyrics. There are successful examples of weak plays being used as the basis for hit musicals—*Oklahoma!* for one. A thin, simple plot can be enhanced with music and dance, but *Pleasures and Palaces* was not to be one of them. It was still a bad show, although it had some beautiful costumes by Freddy Wittop. The one thing I really enjoyed about the show was wearing the costumes.

*Pleasures and Palaces* dealt with John Paul Jones, Catherine the Great, and Potemkin. Two English actors, Hy Hazel and Alfred Marks, were signed to play Catherine and Potemkin. Phyllis Newman and John McMartin were the other leads. These were not exactly big names that would convince people to pay the $9.90 that was the top ticket price that year.

Rehearsals started at Variety Arts, Room 302, and the men were told not to shave because we all needed to have beards. This didn't exactly thrill me because my beard was a bit scraggly. After three days, Eddie Gaspar had a beautiful full beard while I looked like I hadn't shaved that morning. I didn't much like the choreography that Fosse was doing. The opening was a stylized Cossack number, imitating Russian folk dancers, but we weren't Russian and didn't have the spectacular tricks that Russians have. Another number was about happy villagers in a Potemkin village. It had possibilities but was not yet top drawer Fosse. He always came to rehearsals in the morning seemingly knowing what he wanted to do but not always knowing how to get there. His steps usually weren't particularly difficult, but the style was hard to do. More time was spent trying to emulate Bob's style than on the actual steps. Each dancer had to make adjustments because they had different proportions than Bob. Stretch the rib cage, life the chin, you need to be slightly off balance, etc. On the mornings after the first day of rehearsals, dancers would always wake up with sore muscles that they previously hadn't known they possessed. Fosse tried to finish most of the dances before the principals came in because when they arrived he had to focus his time on them and the book rehearsals. While Bob was in another room rehearsing the principals, Merritt would rehearse and clean up the dance numbers. The only time I saw Bob get testy with the company was one day when he had a bad case of dysentery and he was trying to rehearse and run to the john at the same time.

We went to the Fisher Theatre in Detroit to try the show out. We opened to very bad reviews, and the changes began. Almost immediately, Jack Cassidy arrived to replace Alfred Marks. For some reason, Merritt Thompson and Fosse had a falling out, and that was the end of that long-term relationship. Fosse was directing the show as well as doing the choreography. Rumors of fights and disagreements started flying.

Among the numbers Fosse had done for the show was one to the tune of "Tears of Joy" that was rather pedestrian. One day we came to rehearsals and Bob said he was going to re-do the number. He had a new concept and started doing a highly stylized, sophisticated new number. The dancers were excited. After a few bars, we knew that this was going to be a "Fosse" number. A few days later, the number was about half finished, and we were in the middle of rehearsals on the stage when the doors of the auditorium opened unexpectedly. The producers and all of the "big wigs" entered and came down to the stage. As they approached, the sense of doom was palpable. Rehearsal stopped. We all took seats in the auditorium and were told that we were going to close at the end of the week.

This was a shock. I had never done a show that closed out of town, although it was not unusual. With thoughts of the unemployment line, the realization that it was spring and there would be no new shows for several months, the numbness began to settle in. Fosse addressed us saying that he had known that the book was weak, but he thought that he could hide it with "icing on the cake." I had always thought that Fosse thinking he could cover up weaknesses in a show with a lot of icing was his Achilles heel. Years later in *Chicago*, he did a whole number called "Razzle Dazzle" on the subject. Fosse then asked us if we would mind rehearsing the next day because there was some work he wanted to do on "Tears of Joy." That was a request no Fosse dancer would turn down. This man was loved and revered by his dancers.

The next day was remarkable. We gathered at the theater and began rehearsing "Tears of Joy." After a couple of hours, Fosse called it quits, and we sat around talking for a while. At some point, the pianist started playing the music from a previous Fosse show, and any dancer who knew the number started to perform it, then another number, and then another. It was such an afternoon of nostalgia, love, and remembered successes that we were emotionally drained when we finally stopped. That night when we arrived for the final performance, Frank Loesser had left a laundry basket filled with razors and shaving cream at the stage door.

Feuer & Martin, the producers of *Little Me*, had a new show called *Skyscraper* ready for production. Rehearsals were to begin in mid-summer. Auditions were held, and I signed a contract. Then I was also asked to stage *Little Me* for a summer stock production. I wasn't sure about the procedures and legalities. I knew that many dancers from the Broadway production of a show staged shows for summer stock, but it seemed to me that I had no right to give Fosse's choreography to other producers. I knew the choreography, but it belonged to Fosse, and I thought that he ought to get some money for it. I called Fosse and asked if he would object to my doing it. He said to go ahead and do it, that he got his money from a share of the licensing agreements. He told me that I was the first person who had ever asked him for permission to use his choreography. I had scored points.

The summer production of *Little Me* was being shared by three summer stock operations in St. Louis, Pittsburgh, and Indianapolis. Donald O'Connor was going to play Sid Caesar's role. Virginia Martin and Nancy Andrews were going to do their original roles, and there were a couple of other actors in crucial roles who were going to play all three venues.

My job was to go to St. Louis for two weeks to stage all the ensemble numbers during the day while the local company performed *110 in the Shade* at night. The second week, we put the principals into the show while the St. Louis people performed *Here's Love.* As soon as the show opened in St. Louis, I flew to Pittsburgh and staged the show without the principals while the local company performed at night. When the principals finished a week in St. Louis, they flew to Pittsburgh, had an afternoon run through, and learned who was playing which part. The night they opened in Pittsburgh, I went on to Indianapolis where the whole process was repeated, rehearsals during the day while the locals performed *Can Can* with Edie Adams at night.

As the month passed, I got less and less sleep. A week after *Little Me* opened in Indianapolis, rehearsals were set to begin for *Skyscraper* back in New York. I went to Flint to visit Mom for a couple of days. When I walked into her house, I was so thin that she gasped and almost didn't recognize me. I slept most of the next twenty-four hours.

# * Chapter 19 *

*I* cherish Julie Harris. I cherish the name, the star, the talent, the woman, and the love affair I had with her. Don't lick your lips, it wasn't that kind of an affair. When I used to read *The New York Times* in the high school library, I noticed that a woman named Julie Harris kept getting notices in flop shows like *Sundown Beach* and *The Young and Fair.* After I came to New York, she also seemed to be in everything that opened and closed quickly. Then came *The Member of the Wedding* and I, like everyone else, was awed by her performance. Later when she played Sally Bowles in *I Am a Camera*, I absolutely fell in love with her. I saw it eight times from the second balcony of the Empire Theater, and then I saw everything she did, usually at the Actor's Fund performances. I thought Julie was the most wonderful person I had ever seen on stage. After the opening reviews came out, the producers had a ceremony where she was officially anointed a "star," and her name was moved above the title on the marquee of the Empire Theater. I think that was the last time I had ever heard of that being done.

Feuer & Martin had two shows being readied for production, *Skyscraper* and *Walking Happy.* I understood that originally they had planned for Julie Harris to do *Walking Happy* but *Skyscraper* was ready first, so they switched their plans, signing Julie for *Skyscraper.* It was a musical adaptation of Elmer Rice's hit of the Forties called *Dream Girl* about the romance between a woman with romantic fantasies and a newspaper reporter. In the adaptation, not only did the woman have fantasies but she owned a brownstone house that was impeding the construction of a high-rise building. So this time, the romance would be between her and the foreman of the construction crew. Cy Feuer was to direct with Michael Kidd doing the choreography. Peter Stone wrote the book; music and lyrics were by Van Huesen and Cahn and Theoni Aldredge did the costumes. I was going to be in a musical with Julie Harris. I was in seventh heaven.

Don Chastain and Victor Spinelli, who had been a big comic success the previous year in *Oh, What A Lovely War*, were signed to be Julie's leading men. Victor was a "hot" new name, although Don Chastain was not Feuer & Martin's first choice for the leading man. They wanted Peter Marshall, but Peter was signed to do a musical in Los Angeles and could not get out of his contract. However, Feuer & Martin did not believe that Peter's show would be a hit, so they took a gamble. They had production dates to meet, so they started rehearsals with Don. The gamble worked because Peter's show was a flop, and after a couple of weeks into rehearsals, Chastain was fired, and we suddenly had a new leading man, Peter Marshall.

By the first day of principal rehearsals, the ensemble already had been rehearsing for a couple of weeks. I arrived at Variety Arts one morning and rode the elevator to the third floor with a little mouse of a woman in a plain black cotton dress. She was clutching a bound script to her bosom. This unassuming little woman was the effervescent Broadway star, Julie Harris. I can only imagine what she was feeling as she started the unfamiliar course of rehearsing a musical, her first and last. I was dumbstruck to be in an elevator with Julie Harris.

For the first few days, the book was rehearsed in one room while the singers and dancers worked in another. The only time we saw the principals was if we had been assigned to a small part and were called in to do a scene. It was the usual procedure—

the book and the musical numbers were rehearsed separately then slowly brought together as necessary. The first time Julie arrived for the staging of a musical number, she was dressed in ill-fitting black tights and leotards, looking somewhat like a "modern dancer." I think somewhere in her training she had studied a little with Anna Sokolov. She looked like a lost waif amongst the chorus girls with their Danskin tights and leotards pulled up to their hips to make the legs look longer. Julie went shopping and turned up at the next rehearsal with sheer tights pulled up to her hips, and the company's love affair with Julie began.

I had never been in a company in which the star of the show was as adored as was Julie by the *Skyscraper* company. Whatever the future problems with the show, they were all tackled with the idea of helping Julie, protecting Julie, and making Julie a success. She was the heart of the show around which the company coalesced. It was a happy company and all because of Julie. Of course, it didn't hurt that we felt we had a hit on our hands. From the get go, everyone thought that the book was wonderful, the score great, and a "can't miss" show.

We opened the show in Detroit and were very surprised at the notices. They were not good. They didn't like the *Dream Girl* part of the show, although they did like the subplot of the brownstone being in the way of constructing a skyscraper. The rewrites began. Peter Stone, the writer, de-emphasized the *Dream Girl* part and stressed the *Skyscraper* elements of the show. Everyday there were new "sides" to be learned. Sometimes the new scene would just be rehearsed and held in abeyance until it could be put in the show at a later time. Sometimes the new scene would go in that night. It was bedlam. At the end of rehearsal, we would always do a recap of what was "new" for that night and what was to be held for the future. Sometimes scenes were put in the show that made no sense because the next scene, which would pull it together, hadn't been changed yet. Poor Julie was going on stage in scenes she had just learned that afternoon. But she was a rock. One night after the show, she was going over lines with a stage manager and said that she wished that a word was not repeated so much in one particular scene. The stage manager asked her why she didn't complain about it to the director or make a suggestion. She replied, "Oh no, I couldn't do that." She felt that it was not her place, that it was the director's role. I know of no other star who wouldn't use her influence if she were uncomfortable with a line.

A big problem was Victor Spinelli. He wasn't very good and wasn't adding much to the show. The producers had every right to replace him, but he had a "run of the play" contract that meant he would have to be paid until the following June whether he did or did not perform. The solution was to diminish his role to the point that he felt it would do damage to his career and would then ask to be let out of his contract. Each day he had less and less to do and finally asked to be let out. In the meantime, Charles Nelson Reilly had been brought to Detroit and ensconced in the Book-Cadillac Hotel. He was learning the show, including some scenes not being given to Spinelli. Another actor had also been hired to replace Spinelli and rehearse his scenes until Spinelli left. As soon as Spinelli was gone, the second actor was let go, and Charles joined the show. The unlikely duo of Charles Nelson Reilly and Julie Harris became fast friends.

I almost became the first nude on Broadway—well, almost nude. In the number, which closed the first act, Julie was dreaming of all the men who had tried to date her. They emerged from the closet and exited through the window. When she pulled the shower curtain back, I was in the tub wearing a hat and a very small, flesh colored bikini. A transom above the tub opened and a towel would drop from it. I would wrap myself in the towel and chase Julie around the stage. I was ambivalent about the scene. I was very self-conscious, but it also brought me a moment of attention. During that brief time when I was revealed, I could see all the binoculars in the audience trained on me. The number was not very good, and after it received no applause for several performances, it was cut from the show. My moment of glory disappeared, but unfortunately, not before my mom saw it. She came down from Flint with her theater club early one week to see the show. She was also planning to see the show that weekend with my brother and his family. After the show, I met her in the lobby of the Fisher Building. She looked very old and tired. In hindsight, I should have known something was about to happen because that following Friday Jim called to say that Mom had died.

I didn't want to deal with sympathy from the company. I told Phil Friedman the situation and that if nothing new was scheduled to be put in the show on Monday then I would need the day off. Michael Kidd offered me his car, but as I hadn't driven in three or four years, I declined his offer. On Monday morning, I took an early Greyhound bus to Flint arriving in time to visit the funeral home before the ceremony. Afterwards, my oldest brother, Freeman, and I left the dinner early, and he drove me back to Detroit in time for the show. There was so much intrigue going on that some of the company had decided that I had been sent to New York on some devious errand. No one asked any questions.

At this time, the practice of doing extended previews in New York was controversial. The critics contended that when a show came to New York, it should officially open. They allowed a couple of performances for a show to settle into a new theater, but then they wanted to review it. *Skyscraper* was not ready for New York, so the producers faced a dilemma. Should they book the show into another city for a few weeks, which was very expensive, or should they go to New York and face the criticism of extended previews, chancing that someone would review the show before its official opening? After contacting the various newspapers, Feuer & Martin were assured that the newspapers would not send their critics until the opening. The decision was made to go to New York for a month of previews while the show was worked on.

We set up shop at the Lunt-Fontanne Theatre that was owned by Feuer & Martin. About two weeks into previews, word passed through the cast that Dorothy Kilgallen, a powerful newspaper columnist at the time, was in the audience. During the second act, word also passed that she had spent the intermission across the street at Dinty Moore's Restaurant and was soused as usual. The next afternoon during rehearsals, everyone was reading her column in which she blasted the show. We were all furious, feeling that she had double crossed us. A couple of days later during rehearsals word spread that Kilgallen had suddenly died. All of us started to smile then caught ourselves, but we couldn't control the glint in our eyes at the just desserts which had been meted out.

Opening night of *Skyscraper* was wonderful. Everything worked. Everyone was up. It was probably the best performance *Skyscraper* ever had. We got good reviews. It was supposed to be a hit. It wasn't. The competition that year was tough. A few weeks after we opened, *Sweet Charity* opened, and it was a huge hit. Later in the spring, *Mame* with Angela Lansbury was the show to see. We were definitely in the "also-ran" category. For a short while, we played to capacity, but it wasn't long before the audience tapered off. Julie obviously drew her fans who were curious to see her in a musical, but as wonderful as she was, as talented as she was—she couldn't sing. It was a minor flaw in the jewel, but a rather major one in a musical.

Shortly after *Sweet Charity* opened, I received a telephone call backstage just before the performance. It was Fosse. He wondered if I was happy where I was and if I would like to move over and swing *Sweet Charity*. It was certainly a tempting offer, but I've always had a sense of loyalty to the show I was doing. *Skyscraper* was a happy company, and so I regrettably turned Fosse's offer down.

It also didn't help our business that there was a two-week subway strike during our run. Carpools were arranged for the cast that lived in New Jersey, Upper Manhattan, Queens, or

Brooklyn. One woman offered to chauffeur Julie from her home on the East Side, but Julie said she could walk. Traffic was horrific. On matinee days I had to walk to the theater, walk back home to walk the dog between shows, walk back downtown to do the evening show, then walk home after the show. After the subway strike was over, there was a newspaper strike, so publicity and advertising were curtailed. Big hits were not affected, but the marginal shows were hit hard.

One evening I had just started to prepare dinner before walking the dog and going to the theater. Suddenly the lights went out. Figuring that it would be twenty minutes or so before they came back on, I turned off the stove and took the dog out. I walked down to Riverside Park and realized that the situation was pretty serious. There were no lights across the river in New Jersey. The park was filling with people in a party mood. By the time I got home, the lights were still out, so I cooked dinner by candlelight, then set off for the theater expecting that the lights would come on and there could be a show. At the theater, everything was in turmoil, and there was talk of doing the show by candlelight, not a very practical idea. We hung around the theater until about nine o'clock when it was announced that the performance was cancelled. The big blackout of 1965 was later deemed an "Act of God" for which we wouldn't get paid.

One Sunday morning, I was looking through the classified real estate ads. I wanted to move but was in no great hurry. Although I had a rent controlled apartment, I was looking for another one with more space. Buried in an ad for West End Avenue apartments, I found a notice for one on Seventy-Fifth Street. I took a leisurely stroll down to the agency. They told me where the apartment was located. I walked over to 57 West Seventy-Fifth Street then ran back to the agency and contracted for the apartment. Three large rooms, an eat-in kitchen, and rent control! Ninety-five dollars a month.

*Skyscraper* struggled along until June when the closing notice went up. It was an especially sad closing. Julie went to

Italy to make *Reflections in a Golden Eye*. *Skyscraper* remains one of my favorite experiences. Whether she could sing or not, Julie Harris was everything a star should be. I never saw her again, except on stage. I was too shy and afraid she wouldn't remember me to try to see her backstage. I was back to worshipping her from afar.

# * Chapter 20 *

F euer & Martin had *Walking Happy* about to go into production in the late summer for a fall opening. Gossiping with someone in Central Park one afternoon, I learned that *Royal Hunt of the Sun*, which was about to close, was going to do two weeks at the Greek Theatre in Los Angeles. I let them know that I was available. Shortly afterwards, I received a call to join them for the California engagement. A week's rehearsal and two weeks in Los Angeles helped me get through that summer—with a little help from unemployment insurance.

*Walking Happy* was based on the Brighouse play *Hobson's Choice*, the story of a maiden daughter's escape from her tyrannical father through marriage to an illiterate cobbler in the employ of his father. It was adapted by Van Heusen and Cahn. Cy Feuer was to direct, and Danny Daniels was to do the choreography. Fosse was also involved by doing one uncredited number, "Think of Something Else," and some directorial suggestions.

I understand that after Julie Harris was switched to *Skyscraper*, Mary Martin had been signed to do *Walking Happy*, but Miss Martin's husband had died and she was having second thoughts about doing the show. Feuer & Martin, rather than hold her to her contract and have an unhappy star, released her from the contract and started casting again.

George Rose was signed as the father. Norman Wisdom, a British actor who had done *Where's Charlie?*, was signed to star as Will Mussop, the cobbler. Louise Troy was tapped as the daughter. Louise had done supporting roles and done them well, but there was no money in these names. The story was originally about the father and daughter, so the book was immediately out of whack because it made the cobbler the focal point and the star. I would like to have seen Julie Harris do this show. I think she would have had a greater success than she did with *Skyscraper*, and her starring in the show would have made *Walking Happy* work better because the book wouldn't have been skewed to make more of the cobbler's character than it should have been.

After rehearsals at Variety Arts, Room 302, we headed once again for the Fisher Theatre where Shirley Eder, the Detroit critic, asked Louise Troy how she felt about the propensity of Feuer & Martin's leading ladies to disappear, never to be heard from again. It was a rude question but had some validity. Allyn Ann McLerie from *Where's Charlie?* went on to bomb in *Miss Liberty* and faded into obscurity. Susan Johnson disappeared after *Whoop Up*, as did Hildegard Neff after *Silk Stockings*. Isabel Bigley faded away after *Guys and Dolls*, and Virginia Martin faded away after *How to Succeed* and *Little Me*. Julie Harris escaped this fate because she brought a big name with her going in, and Dorretta Morrow had had some success after *Where's Charlie?* Miss Eder did, however, pose an interesting question. I don't know how Louise Troy answered it, but she may have remembered it later in her life.

Danny Daniels, the choreographer, was a talented and nice man, but I think he lacked authority. He had done some good work in previous shows and on television, but he was not A-list like Fosse or Kidd. I think he came to rehearsals with good ideas for the big numbers, but he didn't have many ideas about what to do with the lesser numbers. However, in *Walking Happy*, he created an extraordinary clog dance that stopped the show every night. And he created a nice number for the title song. Originally the *Walking Happy* number was to be performed using the turntable on the stage, but as soon as we got to Detroit and tried it, that idea was dropped, and the number was strictly linear. There was another number with Specters and George Rose in a drunken stupor using fire coming out of their fingers and canes that appeared and disappeared. It was a nice number, though it didn't work as well as the idea. Once one had learned Danny's steps, there wasn't much to do except rehearse them or tinker with them a bit. Unlike Fosse—where learning the steps were only the first part followed by time spent on style, precision, and isolation—Danny did not ask a great deal in the way of style.

In every show there is a number that is rehearsed to death before it finally dies. It's rehearsed so much because it isn't working and probably never will, so it's tinkered with for days upon days, and still it will never work. Fosse is the one choreographer with whom I have worked who does this and then one day chucks the whole thing and starts over with a new approach, usually successfully. We had such a number in *Walking Happy*, and whenever there wasn't anything else to work on, we would rehearse it. One day we were called on stage to rehearse it yet again. There were no changes, just more rehearsal. I overheard Burt Bier say, "Oh, it looks like polish time." Marian Haraldson, who was standing next to him, then asked one of the most succinct questions I have ever heard. "How do you polish a turd?"

*Walking Happy* opened in New York in November 1966, and unlike *Skyscraper*, it did not have a brilliant opening. It was downright dull with no spark and no energy. It received nice, but not "box office," reviews. *The Apple Tree* had opened just a week before we did, and *Cabaret* had also opened about the same time. *Cabaret* was a huge hit. We were strictly in the "also ran" category. Unfortunately, as soon as the show opened, it started running longer. At the beginning of the run, the curtain came down about 11:10 p.m., but a month later it was coming down around 11:30 p.m. That is the time at which overtime pay for stagehands begins. Norman was improving the show, adding "business" and "pauses." Sometimes it seemed that even his pauses had pauses embedded within them. Every week a rehearsal would be called, and Cy Feuer would try to speed up the show. After a rehearsal, the show would be ten minutes shorter, but during the week it would lengthen again, so much so that we were afraid to hold the opening curtain for more than a couple of minutes for fear that we would finish after 11:30 p.m., overtime time. The only good thing going for us was the spectacular clog dance, which was an exciting number and stopped the show every night. We did it on the *Ed Sullivan Show* and the *Perry Como Show.* This helped us to survive a little longer.

After the "blue laws" were lifted, Broadway started to have Sunday performances. Before that, Broadway was dark on Sunday. As soon as the "blue laws" were repealed even stores began to open. Shows that were not sold out hits started cancelling Monday night performances instead giving Sunday afternoon shows. For performers with families, it was a terrible schedule, but I liked it. It gave me two nights and almost two days off. It was also a good schedule for *Walking Happy* because it was a family friendly show. The Sunday afternoon show did the best business of the week, so coupled with the rest of the weekend, we were not only surviving, but business was growing. Unfortunately, when business earlier had not been so good and it looked like we would be closing the show at the beginning of summer, Feuer & Martin had agreed to take it to the West Coast for the summer under the aegis of the Los Angeles Light Opera. So even though business was improving, we had to close.

However, before we closed the show in New York, we did the clog number on the Tony Awards show, which was being televised for the first time that year, and it was a great publicity gimmick. All of the musicals did a number from their shows. The Tony awards show was a great success, but *Walking Happy* did not win any awards. It was the year of *Cabaret*.

Before leaving for the Coast, we replaced the leading lady, Louise Troy, with Anne Rogers. Anne was the original Julie Andrews. She had been the leading lady in *The Boy Friend* when it was first done in England. When Feuer & Martin brought the show to the United States, the English producers would not release Anne to re-create the role on Broadway so Julie Andrews was brought over in her stead. Of course, Andrews became a big star and Rogers was left wondering "what might have been"— even though it probably wouldn't have been. Anne replaced Julie Andrews in *My Fair Lady*, and Edwin Lester used her in several of his West Coast shows where she created a bit of a name for herself. Lester insisted that she replace Louise Troy for name value on the West Coast tour. We moved to the Curran Theatre in San Francisco and then to the Dorothy Chandler at the Music Center in Los Angeles. By this time, Los Angeles had built a Performing Arts Center, and shows no longer played the Baptist Church auditorium downtown.

Near the end of the run, I auditioned for Mitzi Gaynor's nightclub act. I didn't have much hope of getting it because it was staged by Ernie Flatt. Ernie, like Agnes de Mille, wouldn't touch me. I had met Ernie socially, and he was always highly complimentary, but he wouldn't hire me. A couple of times at his auditions, he stopped the audition and had me do his combinations by myself. Then he would tell everyone that he wanted them to do the steps like I did. Afterwards, he would hire those who did the steps the way I did while I was shown the door with the ubiquitous "thank you." Once while he was doing *Your Hit Parade* in New York on television, I was recommended as a replacement and Ernie said that I was a fine dancer, but what would the producers think if he showed them my photograph? I was certainly no Adonis, but I didn't think I was ugly. By the time of the Gaynor auditions, I was looking like the guy with the toupee. Gaynor was very nice and friendly, but again Ernie asked me to demonstrate his steps while wondering about one of the other dancers from *Walking Happy*. He described the dancer and mentioned that he thought he was very handsome. I told him the dancer's name, although I wanted to say, "Oh, you mean the one who looks like you?" There was a decided resemblance. The next day, Gaynor's husband, Jack Bean, called. He was very nice in telling me that I wasn't what they were looking for. They hired the "look-alike."

# * *Chapter 21* *

By the mid-sixties, the convergence of New York City demographics, the divestiture of movie chains from the movie studios, and the changing tastes in music had had a deleterious effect on Times Square and the theater. Since the Second World War, the middle class had been moving out of New York into homes in the suburbs. That middle-class audience was no longer a short subway or bus ride from Times Square. Middle class retail operations had also changed with the loss of customers. Stern's department store moved out of New York. Macy's went upscale and survived. Gimbel's went downscale then closed. The newspapers followed suit. The upscale *New York Times* and the blue collar *Daily News* survived as did the only afternoon paper, the *New York Post*, which was as detested by conservatives for its liberal editorial policy as it is detested today by liberals for its conservative views. The other papers closed or merged then closed. The *World-Telegram*, already a merged newspaper, merged again and became the *World-Telegram-Sun*, but did not last long in that format. The same happened with the *Journal-American* when it merged with the *Tribune*. The *PM*, the *Mirror*, and the *Brooklyn Eagle* had already gone under. With the disappearance of daily newspapers came the disappearance of the theater critics who could make or break a show. Instead of a possible three to four split of pans to raves, or something in between, the theater was left with three critics with a much more finite possibility of split decisions. With those newspapers gone, all that newspaper space that needed to be filled with columns of print vanished. Press agents had less chance to get their shows mentioned in columns because there was less space for anecdotal stories about their shows and stars.

With the divestiture of the movie chains from the movie studios, the studios no longer had to keep their theaters filled with new product. Television was also competing for the theater audiences, and the great movie palaces began to come down. The Paramount, Roxy, and Capitol were razed and replaced with office buildings. The Astor had its seats removed and became a flea market. The movies started having premiers at smaller East Side theaters. The remaining Times Square movie houses made do with sexploitation and soft porn movies so the nightly crowds in Times Square went from middle class to sleazy and seemed dangerous to suburbanites. The only first class hotel in Times Square, the Astor, was eventually torn down and replaced by an office building, so tourists or business people no longer stayed in Times Square. It would be some years before Mickey Mouse and Walt Disney rediscovered Times Square. In the meantime, theater suffered.

Tucked away in the side streets off Times Square, the legitimate theaters were trying to survive. For musicals, however, there was another problem. Musical tastes were changing—rock music was becoming popular. Musicals usually recorded their shows within weeks of opening, rushing the recordings into production hoping that there would be a hit recording to draw people into the theater. Frequently one of the big popular vocalists like Tony Bennett would record a couple of songs from a show, but with changing musical tastes, there were fewer programs playing that kind of music. Another source of publicity was drying up.

The 1967-1968 season was a dud. Does anyone remember

those wonderful musicals like *How Now Dow Jones*, *The Happy Time*, *Darling of the Day*, *The Education of H\*Y\*M\*A\*N K\*A\*P\*L\*A\*N*, or *I'm Solomon*? Broadway was changing, and I was getting older. I wasn't really aware of getting older, and I doubt that Broadway was aware that it was changing, but things were different.

Fosse was looking towards Hollywood and films. He had already directed *Lenny* and was now preparing for the movie version of *Sweet Charity*. Big names like Michael Kidd, Onna White, and Agnes de Mille had not been announced for any shows. Now there were new names like Michael Bennett, Ron Fields, and Lee Theodore doing the choreography for the new shows. These choreographers were all people who had emerged from the ensembles of earlier musicals. They usually had their own group of dancers with whom they surrounded themselves, and they were younger. Perhaps these new choreographers were self-conscious about commanding their own peer group, but for whatever reason, except for their assistants, they usually hired a younger group of dancers. It could also be that the older dancers didn't particularly want to work for someone with whom they had worked alongside in ensembles. Whatever the reasons, there was a new group taking command and a younger group being hired.

After finishing *Walking Happy* on the West Coast, I got back to New York too late to even think about the first batch of shows for the coming season. There wasn't much happening anyway. Things were looking rather grim for me financially, but finally in November something turned up, a musical version of *East of Eden* called *Here's Where I Belong*, one of the dullest titles for a musical that I had ever run across. Did it tell you anything about the show or make you want to rush out and buy a ticket or pique your curiosity in any way?

Mitch Miller was the producer. The book was by Terrence McNally, the music and lyrics by Robert Waldman and Alfred Uhry, and Hanya Holm did the choreography. The director of the show was a new "wunderkind" named Michael Kahn. The cast featured Paul Rogers, Nancy Wickwire, James Coco, Walter McGinn, Heather MacRae, and Ken Kercheval. Obviously, this cast wasn't going to sell tickets on name value. The show was going to have to get brilliant reviews and sell itself.

I was curious, but not excited, to work for Hanya Holm. Coming out of the Mary Wigman School of Modern Dance, she was one of the pioneers of the modern dance movement in the United States. In 1948, she hit the big time doing the choreography for *Kiss Me Kate*. It was one of her disciples, Martha Wilcox, who was my first dance instructor at the University of Denver. The word was that concepts were Hanya's, but the steps were created by her assistants, Ray Harrison in the case of *Kiss Me Kate* and later David Nillo for *My Fair Lady*. There was a lot of improvisation. I never liked improvisation and walked out of several auditions when I was asked to do them. As far as I was concerned, the steps were the choreographer's business, not mine. Mine was to do the steps that the choreographer created. I was once at an audition where the "auditionees" were asked to walk through an imaginary cube filled with honey. First of all, you would not be able to breathe, so how could you walk? If you want me to walk slowly with lots of resistance, show me what you want, and I'll try to emulate it. If I can't, don't hire me, but spare me the sophistry.

By the time of *Here's Where I Belong*, Hanya was up in years, probably in her seventies, and no longer danced. Perforce, she had to speak about what she wanted and her assistant, Joe Nelson, would do something, and Hanya would say, "That's correct" or "Change it." She was a delight to work for, always pleasant with no temper. I liked and respected her, but unfortunately, what she was doing was dull as dishwater.

In one number where townspeople were wandering through the village square, I counted eight counts of eight. No one knew exactly what they were doing, and every time we restarted the number, we had to start from the beginning. One day, Joe Nelson asked if anyone knew a place from somewhere in the middle of the number where we could pick up. I told him that on the sixty-fourth count of eight, I was entering from the left, while Paul had just come in from the right, and so and so was in the center doing something. The pianist flipped through the music, counted out the bars, and from then on that was where we started. It must have saved five minutes every time we picked up at that point. I always counted the music.

The book rehearsals were going equally as slowly. It was the first musical for the director, Michael Kahn, and the two stars, Paul Rogers and Nancy Wickwire. By the time we left for Philadelphia and the tryout, the second act had not been completely staged. Paul Rogers, an Englishman, had a trained—if not singing—voice, and was going to be fine. Nancy Wickwire, who had worked primarily off Broadway, was the other star in a supporting role. Why she was hired, I do not know. She wasn't a "name," and although she had a good reputation off Broadway, she was not a musical performer. It seemed that someone was trying to make her a star. We all waited with anticipation during the first run through of the show to see the big scene in which she had to sing a song. It was embarrassing, but the company applauded dutifully, and the big important people all looked pleased with her and themselves. The show itself was disjointed. Everyone said this should be an opera, not a musical. There were four or five different plot lines—a love story, a sibling rivalry, a father/son relationship, a mother/son relationship, and a mother/father relationship. It was all too complicated for a musical. Justice was not to be done to any of the plot lines. We would have had a better chance if we concentrated on a couple of plots and got rid of the rest.

Near the end of rehearsals for what I knew was going to be a flop, I received a call from Fosse who was in Hollywood about to begin filming *Sweet Charity* with Shirley MacLaine. Bob asked if I could come to the Coast the next week to do the film. I sure wanted to do so, but there was no way I could get out of my contract to leave for the coast on time. I had to turn down the film to stay in *Here's Where I Belong*. We all knew the fate of the show, but the "powers" all seemed to be enthusiastic.

The first day in Philadelphia, I was walking to the Shubert Theatre with a singer, Pat Kelly. As we approached the theater, we looked up at the marquis that read "Paul Rogers and Nancy Wickwire in *Here's Where I Belong*." Pat said it all when she asked, "Who? Where? In what?"

When we opened, the reviews were as bad we had expected. The heavy conferences amongst the creators began. Obviously, big changes were coming. At first the big changes consisted of a word here and a word there, only fine tuning when what we needed was a complete overhaul. It's in this situation when the professionals were separated from the dilettantes. Unfortunately, we had mostly dilettantes, but finally a big change was announced. Hanya was fired, and Tony Mordente was brought in as her replacement. Musicals in trouble frequently fire the choreographer. It is sometimes a change in the right direction but usually doesn't get at the root of the problem. That would be true in both cases here.

Immediately, Tony started on a new piece to replace Hanya's big dance number about migrant workers. Hanya's dance had been dull and unfocused. At one point, Walter McGinn, playing the James Dean role, joined us and did a *pas de deux* with one of the girls. Walter hurt his back, and I started replacing him in that number. It made no difference—it was a subplot that went nowhere, and the audience was unaware of any change. Tony's number, at least, had some energy in it and got a reaction from the audience.

In the meantime, the midnight conferences went on and on. A few words were changed here and there. The stage manager, Bill Dodds, was a friend of mine, and he clued me in on the conferences. A lot of time was taken discussing me—they hated my toupee. Apparently, I was what was wrong with the show. Finally, one night, the hairdresser brought in a cheap wig and put it on me. They liked it so much that by the following week all the men had wigs. It was a simple solution that had taken them a couple of weeks to make. Another quick solution would have been to fire me and get on with the really important matters. I'm not sure, but I think neither Hanya nor Tony would have agreed to that because I was one of only a couple of reliable male dancers they had.

In the midst of all this chaos, there was one fine experience, Graciela Daniele. Graciela was the Argentine dancer who had just come to the States. I was usually partnered with her, and she was a joy to dance with. There was such great communication and interplay when dancing with the great Graciela. I am particularly pleased that she has since had such great success as a choreographer and director.

One day while talking with one of the female dancers, she said that the others were asking why I still danced. Was it because I still enjoyed it? The question started to lurk in my mind. Dancers have a shelf life. Most stop dancing at forty, and I was almost there. How long could I continue dancing? And what was I going to do when I stopped dancing? Her question gave me an insight into what others thought of me, and it was a bit disturbing. I had tried to move into acting, but agents thought of me as a dancer, so few would put me up for an acting part. The few auditions I had had were not successful. One gets typecast as an ensemble person. Barbara Sharma quit dancing and said it took two years before agents began to stop thinking of her as a dancer. It was a problem that I was going to have to face. The proverbial handwriting was on the wall.

We finished in Philadelphia and moved to New York for a month of previews at the Billy Rose Theater on Forty-First Street, the southernmost theater still in use on Broadway. The Billy Rose was one of my favorite theaters from an audience viewpoint because it was medium sized and had great sight lines. However, its location was not in one of the prime spots, so if you played there, you had better be a big hit because there was no walk-in business on Forty-First Street. It was another bad omen—as if we needed more.

The show had probably improved, but not by much. We were still dealing with too many plot lines for only two and a half hours with music and dance. Our audiences were mostly "paper," free tickets given out to Actor's Equity and other organizations in order to partially fill the house so we wouldn't be playing to an empty theater, which is really demoralizing.

In the number with an infinite number of counts of eight, I wore a postman's uniform complete with mailbag. One day, Tony Mordente told me not to wear the mailbag that was kept on the prop table. It was a prop as far as I was concerned, and in the structure of departments in the theater, I left it on the prop table. A couple of days later, the stage manager called me to his desk and said that the costume designer, Ruth Morley, had said that I had screamed at her "like a banshee." I was dumbfounded. I had spoken with Ruth only in passing and had never had an argument or an acrimonious conversation with her. She was objecting to my not wearing the mailbag. I told her to speak to Tony—if Tony did not want me to wear it, I wouldn't wear it. If he did want me to wear it, I would. As far as I was concerned it was a prop and out of her jurisdiction, but I took my orders from Tony. Now that my toupee wasn't ruining the show, it was the presence or absence of the mailbag. Well, when you're heading for disaster, strange things become important. I never discovered why she had taken this tack. I had never heard that she was a nasty woman, so her accusation remains a mystery to me.

We had our opening on a Sunday night. Michael Kahn wrote me an appreciative note about my performance, which I took to be something of an apology for making me the focus of all those production meetings. We gave the usual enthusiastic performance knowing that we were doomed but still hoping for a miracle. Could we possibly be better than we thought? Virginia Martin, who had taken care of my dog during all those rehearsals, came with me to the opening night party, although the party started breaking up as soon as the reviews were out. We were not better than we thought. The next day I arrived at the theater to find that our opening had also been our closing. Pick up your makeup box and go home. Without being aware of it, I had given my last performance on Broadway. It had been a dreary season on Broadway, and it was not until a couple of months later that finally a couple of hit musicals would open— *George M* and *Hair*.

A few weeks later, dear Hanya had a party for the dancers. Terrance McNally, who had had his name taken off the credits, was there and said that Mexicans should have picketed the show because of the depiction of Mexicans in the big dance number. I didn't remind him that we were once picketed by Asian actors because his friend, James Coco, was cast as a Chinese servant.

# * Chapter 22 *

---

M y next disaster started in the late summer of 1968. It was called *A Mother's Kisses*. It was by Bruce Jay Friedman, adapted from his book, with music and lyrics by Richard Adler. Gene Saks directed. Onna White did the choreography. Saks and White had worked as a team on *Mame*, which was a huge success. Bea Arthur, Saks's wife, had been a big success in a supporting role in *Mame* and was cast as the leading lady. A young actor, Bill Calaway (remember him?), was cast as her son. Bernadette Peters who had won great reviews in *George M* was a featured player. Most of the ensemble were close to twenty years of age. I was hired to swing the show and to be an assistant stage manager.

The story of *A Mother's Kisses* was about an overly possessive mother but was not ripe material for a musical. Like Momma Rose in *Gypsy*, she could fascinate you, but there was no way you were going to like her. She was a beast. To make a musical out of this material would take very deft hands, which we didn't have, although we did have some nice music and Onna White who could build a good number from some simple steps and a lot of repetition.

We rehearsed the show at the 46th Street Theatre, where we would play when we opened in New York, and at the Lunt-Fontanne Theatre across the street. The going was slow. Michael

Kahn with *Here's Where I Belong* was a speed demon compared to Gene Saks who had actual experience with musicals. The first few scenes were staged and rehearsed, then staged and rehearsed again, then restaged, rehearsed, and rewritten. We never seemed to move ahead. For an hour a day, Onna exercised Bea Arthur. Onna had trimmed and conditioned Angela Lansbury for *Mame* and was trying to do the same for Bea, but it didn't work. Bea was a big, horsey woman, and even after all that conditioning, she remained a big, horsey woman. She seemed to have but one note—outrage—in her repertoire. A glorious note it was, but it worked better in a supporting role than in a star part.

The day finally came when the cast met on Forty-Sixth Street to take a chartered bus to New Haven to begin the tryout. We learned when we took roll call that Bernadette Peters had been fired. Her makeup kit had already been shipped to New Haven and had to be returned to New York. Bernadette was the one breath of fresh air in the show, and her firing was an ominous note, as if we needed any more ominous notes.

We opened in New Haven to terrible reviews. I had been in shows where the rumor of people walking out was prevalent backstage, but it was never noticeable. With *A Mother's Kisses*, it was quite obvious. When the curtain went up on the second act, we could see big gaps in the audience where people had been sitting during the first act. Eddie Gaspar, who was doing the choreography for *The Fig Leaves Are Falling* and was to follow us into the Shubert Theatre came up to see the show. He did not have one word of encouragement. When you're in a bomb, you like to hear that "there are some good things in the show," "nothing that's not fixable," or "it needs tightening." Eddie offered no hope whatsoever. We were a very depressed company that traveled on to Baltimore for a month at the Mechanic Theatre.

The show also received bad notices in Baltimore. Why wouldn't it? It hadn't changed appreciably despite constant rehearsals and rewrites. One thing had changed, and it was the sociability of the company. Usually on a tryout tour the company gathers in some bar to wind down from the day. Not with *A Mother's Kisses.* The younger members of the company were a different generation and had discovered the joys of smoking pot. After the show, they disappeared for private parties. I think that during our week in New Haven and two weeks in Baltimore, I never once saw the company gather in public after the show. I wasn't positive, but I thought I had figured out why I was never invited—either I was too old, or they recognized my streak of Puritanism.

In Baltimore, we continued the futile rehearsing and rewriting. Rumors abounded that this or that "play doctor" was in the audience, probably diagnosing a terminal patient. No one seemed to come up with any suggestions about how to improve the show. By the fourth week, the ultimate rumor began wafting through the theater. This one turned out to be true. We were closing in Baltimore. It was a depressing train ride back to New York.

In the spring, *1776* was announced and auditions were held. It didn't sound promising to me, but Peter Stone from *Skyscraper* was the writer, and Robert Tucker, who I knew, was to be the choreographer, so I thought I had a chance at a job. At the audition, after we danced, we were all asked to read. After I had read, the stage manager, with whom I had read, said, "Sterling reading" and asked that I not accept another job without letting *1776* know. I left the audition elated and pretty sure I had a new job, but they never called.

Later, I auditioned for the Las Vegas company of *Mame* starring Susan Hayward. At the final lineup, we were asked if anyone was willing to swing the show, and I said I was willing if the salary was negotiable. I thought that learning all the roles was worth more than minimum salary. When I talked to the office, I told them I wanted fifty dollars over minimum and never heard back from them.

When I first started auditioning for Broadway shows, I got

nowhere, then I started getting closer, and then I was pretty assured of a job before I walked in. Now I seemed to be in a new phase, and it was not comforting. There were not a lot of jobs to be had, and I was having trouble landing those that were available. Carol Haney was gone. Fosse was concentrating on movies and had nothing on his plate for Broadway. Feuer & Martin were not producing anything. The "Golden Age of Broadway" seemed to be over, at least for me.

One show finally turned up. It was *1491* by Meredith Wilson, to be produced on the West Coast for the Los Angeles Civic Light Opera. Danny Daniels was to do the choreography, and I was hired as swing dancer and assistant stage manager. Like most shows produced by the Los Angeles Civic Light Opera, it was announced that the show would go to New York after the West Coast engagement. I doubted that it would though because most of those shows died in California. I wasn't any more encouraged after I read the script. The stars of the show were John Cullum as Columbus, Jean Fenn as Queen Isabella, and Chita Rivera, who was now based on the West Coast raising her daughter, as Columbus's lady friend.

While *George M* played downstairs at the Dorothy Chandler Pavilion, we rehearsed *1491* upstairs. As assistant stage manager and swing dancer, I spent most of my time in the dancing rehearsals and saw little of the book rehearsals. When the time came to put the show together, I was pleasantly surprised. I found it interesting and started to think this was not just another Light Opera production. I even started to think we might make it to New York, which would be great.

We moved to Pasadena for a week to set the show up, doing technical and costume rehearsals. Then somehow the show I'd liked disappeared, never to be seen again. I didn't know if this was a case of it being over produced or not, but the show that I had found interesting in rehearsal had been lost, and I had no idea where it went. Wherever it went, it took any hopes of going to New York with it. It was as dreary as I had originally thought it would be.

Bad reviews for the Los Angeles engagement were followed by more bad reviews for the San Francisco run at the Curran Theatre. One night after the show in San Francisco, I went to the bar across the street. I felt a tap on my shoulder and turned around to find Rod Alexander. He had disappeared from the theater world after his divorce from Bambi Linn. Whenever his name had come up, no one had heard of or from him, nor did I learn that evening where he had been or what he had been doing. We spent the night closing the bars and "laying one on," but he was reticent about his activities. No matter, it was great seeing him that night, though I never saw or heard of him again. I hope he's well. He is one of my favorite people and was instrumental in getting my career started.

*1491* closed on December 18, 1969, just in time for me to get home for Christmas. For me, the closing night was memorable only because one of the dancers didn't show up for the matinee or evening shows. Evidently he had gone home early, which necessitated my going on for him. For two performances, I had to be the top man on a human pyramid without having rehearsed. Somehow I managed it without falling and breaking my back. Although I didn't know it at the time, that would be my last performance at the Curran Theatre.

I stayed in San Francisco for a couple of days because my hotel was paid to the end of the month, and I was in no hurry to get home. The writing was on the wall—adjustments needed to be made in my life. The choreographers that I had relied upon to do a show every year weren't working as much. My producers weren't producing. There were fewer shows being done, and the new guard was taking over from the old guard. I was about to turn thirty-nine and obviously wouldn't be able to dance much longer. I hadn't been able to transition into acting, and there wasn't a lot of opportunity for me to get jobs as an assistant stage manager because there was little activity on the Broadway scene.

Back in New York with no job and without any planning or forethought, I enrolled in a school for computer programming, a profession about which I knew nothing but had heard was the up and coming area of employment. The school was a racket. I took an aptitude test, and, before I was done with it, the instructor judged it to be remarkable. I wondered at the time if I had actually finished the test if it would have been judged astounding? The class was full of dullards. I didn't feel that I was much better, and that I had probably wasted the student loan that I had taken. Those student loans were a boon to the school. They were almost a part of the registration form. The school had a student, and the student had a debt. The instructors were as dull as the students.

However, someone or something was watching over me. Near the end of the course, through a friend, I got an interview for a trainee position at a bank, and miraculously I got the job. I think my having a job raised my grade to an A+ at the school. That must have been the reason because I sure wasn't doing A+ work, although I did manage to beat one of their other applicants for the job.

So, without quitting showbiz, I had quit showbiz. Although I wasn't happy about it, somehow it felt appropriate. Many circles had been completed. I'd made it from Brown City to Broadway. In my first Broadway show, Chita Rivera had been the understudy for the star. In my last Broadway show, Chita was the star. I had seen the world and had had a lot of fun along the way. I danced with and for the best performers of my generation.

On with the show!

# AFTERWORD

_____

Gene Gavin (nee Herbert Eugene Tuttle, my uncle) left the bright lights of Broadway theater to work in a bank about the time I moved to New York City. Sadly, I never saw him perform but he introduced me to Broadway, taking me to *Follies*, *Hello Dolly*, *Mame*, *A Chorus Line*, *Company*, *Pippin*, and others.

He lived for the rest of his life in the same rent-controlled apartment at 75th and Columbus, watching the neighborhood gentrifying around him. For a few years he spent the summers on Fire Island. After he retired from the bank, he learned to speak Spanish and travelled several times to South America.

Later he spent more time in Central Park perched on his favorite bench in the Tupelo Meadow of the Ramble, listening to an ancient transistor radio, doing crossword puzzles from *The New York Times*, chatting with his park buddies and watching the bird watchers watching the birds.

One of the great joys of his later years was Dancers Over 40, a group of retired dancers in New York. On our frequent phone calls, he would excitedly tell me about their meetings and the column he wrote for the group's newsletter.

Gene started to call me for word processing advice so I asked him what he was writing. He was vague and said that I could read it someday but that day didn't come until he bequeathed his manuscript to me after his death. *Twinkle Toes* is the edited version of what he wrote about his life as a young man coming to New York with nothing but a dream.

Gene passed away in 2015 after a fall in his apartment, a cruel twist of fate for a dancer who had danced all over the world.